All this is mine

Antony J Stowers

I wrote the first drafts of this just after leaving London to return to my home town of Darlington, northern England, in the autumn of 1994 at the end of an eventful nine years in the capital and returned to the MS occasionally afterwards, fine-tuning and scraping away superfluous vocabulary or dead metaphors, refining it to try to find an original voice. I can do no better than this version, composed in a dirty, cold, empty attic with a perpetually half-full, cracked coffee cup on the left of the keyboard and a thousand cigarette stubs in an ashtray on the other.

All this . . . is based on places I lived and worked or real people I knew after moving to London in 1985. The story itself is broken down into 24 short scenes spread over a few days. It is also a theatre play called 'The Next Life' and was given a reading by The Actors Centre North East at Newcastle Arts Centre in February 2005.

The young man in the story, a Class-A drug dealer called Rob Barlow, is neck-deep in this highly lucrative but dangerous business. Money is designed to buy things, yet it seems that Rob, who has thousands of pounds lying around his unfurnished luxury apartment in London's Chalk Farm, only uses money to make more money and though he lives in a world where everything has an over-inflated price, he exists on less than the essentials: drugs, cigarettes, rent, beer, taxis and luck. He has no friends - only customers and they need him to supply the drugs and take the risks they daren't. Emotional contact is reduced to brief sexual exchanges, human contact is voices on telephones and, when one of them starts threatening him, his illusory world closes in and customers close their doors one by one.

The concept of a floating, invisible observer drifting around London and mixing with a diverse tapestry of various social classes is a great vehicle to explore post-Thatcher decadence in action in British society with a 'Now that we've got all this money, what shall we spend it on?' starting point.

I lived and wrote about these things at a certain period of British history so I'm not pretending to be a philosopher with any great insights to offer. I was just there.

I

I've found I can manipulate not by speaking but by shutting up. I mean is that the sign of a sad case or what? Begging for drugs? Begging for money is one thing, begging for food another, but begging for drugs? For fucks sake! People in London - too much to say and most of it not much use. Really they're bored see? Kidding themselves that 'cause they live in London – even though they don't do fuck all - they must by their sheer presence be leading interesting lives. But really they're desperate, for something to talk about and something to do and they run around ragged and ravaged, pissed and stoned trying to escape that truth. The here and now concerns me. It was Marco the Italian doing the begging. He'd started grovelling for credit at The Durham Arms.

'My friend, can you -?' 'You're a real mate, could I -', 'Friday! I can sort you Friday night!' in the face of silence turn into: 'Sorry!' and 'You're right, you're right, I'm a fool!' and 'It doesn't matter!'

Instead of encouraging people to talk to resolve their problems, we should encourage them to shut their gobs. Silence is a weapon.

Splintered thoughts lap at his imagination like bank-side flotsam as Ahmed's taxi pounces between cars pumping through Camden's clogged veins. Market day, the pavements straddled by stalls and pedestrians.

And tourists and rock and roll rebellion, maaaaan! All the bullshit that makes me hate the whole fucking pack o' you! Repackaging the past? Regurgitating the past more like - Carnaby Street: what the fuck's that all about then? What about the mundane? Don't lie. People don't come here to relish any 'Spirit of London'. People come here to get fucked. They consume drugs copiously in their own towns, cities and countries so London's just another filling station, no, let me re-phrase that: it's King of the Filling Stations. They frequent the bars, clubs, pubs and cafes, sniffing for brain-fucking substances. I'm invisible me, not recognised but known. When regulars drop hints: 'Someone will be in soon' is my cue.

Two whispered requests: one from a source he can't see and one from Marco. He walks into the Gents. A fat biker aiming at the blocked steel trough pisses up the wall and over the floor. He locks himself in the only cubicle. Rock music and chat briefly go up in volume as the Gents' door opens and closes. There is a knock. He opens it and lets Marco in. Marco gives him a twenty. He gives Marco the E and change. Marco pops the E into his mouth, pulls the toilet chain, winks to say thanks and lets himself out.

I try to find words to describe things, how I feel, but drugs have looted me vocab.

Cradled on the precise engineering of the car's German suspension, rocked, gently rocked, seduced by upholstery and pinned in by shafts of sunlight stabbing the interior, his brain computes.

I'll make about a grand this weekend. Coke and E's mainly. Coke's sixty a gram or eighty, depending on how much you look like you can afford. E's are fifteen. It's pills and powders, man. They're the fashion and I'm a dedicated follower of that. In the drug world pills and powders carry status; they divide you into a different social class. And the younger they are the more they're affected by fashions and trends. Youth is the target market - suckled on a diet of credit, allowances and student loans and far, far less faith in a technological future than their Mums and Dads. It's those summer holidays: six weeks with millions of you surfing the idle tide of parties, raves and clubs from July to September - a punishing schedule. I'm from up north by the way, Henrietta. Nothing ever happened there until two-four, oh-one, six-five.

The mobile purrs and he lifts it out, presses the power-window switch and puts the 'phone to his ear as the breeze rushes in.

The day has begun.

II

I'll tell you something for free: the worst word a man can hear in his life is 'No' and I still don't see how the essence of the word is supposed to change anything. Don't things change anyway?

Idle times like these I need a Time Machine to visit the forests of northern Europe when Attila was around, see them vandals swarming like locusts through the civilized world, smashing everything in a wake of desolation. Empires fall. They always fall, like winter follows autumn. I love imagery. I learned it at school: me mates beating themselves up with algebra and equations and me watching a seagull fly between the buildings like a sliver of melting snow and the glint of sun on a distant car.

He crosses the tree-lined street, a tastefully crumbling Victorian terrace, tucked away from the traffic by pines. He opens the gate and glances up to the windows of the first floor where the Laura Ashley curtains tremble.

Joe's on a mobile - Mobile Joe: peddler of all drugs. He come round last week to try a new batch of skunk, eyes like fucking telescopes, we got hammered, I passed out and he went home, end of that one, but next morning 'phone rings bright and early.

'I had six bags when I come to your gaff and now I've only four. We only smoked one so there's one missing. You've fucking nicked it, you thieving Northern cunt!'

Abuse cascades within abuse and rolls down the telephone line for a minute.

'What you on, Joe?' I say when he stops.

'I done some bad horse is all!' Joe stammers.

Noddy of Nuremburg - meet Adolf of Toy Town. All the parts were written out long ago, Joe, just waiting for the actors to come along and speak them on cue. Three days pass by and then Joe turns up on the doorstep full of apologies. To make up we went down Wandsworth to play pool with a Rasta who liked skunk.

As he steps into the flat, Kate floats across and pecks him on the cheek.

'How are things?' she asks in a way that doesn't expect a reply of great depth.

He turns to Ben whose blue eyes float in watery sockets.

'Come in. Sit down. Chill out.'

Drifts into the living room where a thirty-two inch wide-screen stereo spits out words with a velvet tongue.

'After taking the drug she drank copious amounts of water – just as experts advised – but it did little good and she fell quickly into a coma.'

Kate flicks the remote and mutes it.

There's a soft hiss as the beige leather sofa envelops his body and Kate pulls up a matching swivel chair to the glass-topped coffee table, on it a Sheryl Crow CD cover, the transparent plastic cover of a biro to use as a straw and a digital weighing machine. He brings out the stash and puts it on the table. Ben sits next to him.

'Great to see you! How have you been keeping?'

Punters try to seek common ground with their dealers like its part of the ritual to pretend to like their personality but really a man's trade don't enter it; it's all down to chemistry see? But I guess pretending helps people come to terms with the ugliness of what they're about to do to their bodies. But Ben and me go back a way.

'Still flogging space, Ben?'

'Got a little scheme going on at Canary Wharf.'

Opens a small plastic bag, places it carefully on the weighing machine and tips out coke, numbers clocking up silver grey on the LED. Ben squints.

'Go,'

Taps the packet

'Go,'

And again

'Stop.'

Looks at the digits.

'Two hundred'

Ben produces a brown calfskin wallet from which he slides a plastic Gold Card that Kate takes and expertly separates enough powder onto the CD to carve three short fat lines. Ben hands over four fresh fifties. Kate snorts up a line and tosses back her blonde mane, pinching her nose and blinking tears.

'Well?'

'Not bad,' she says, drawing in breath, eyes widening.

Didn't say that half as enthusiastically as you did when we first met Katie, but then again two hundreds' only an hour's kick in the shin these days isn't it?

Ben takes the plastic tube, lifts the CD to his face, sticks one end of the tube into his left nostril and snorts up the second. Kate stands, stretching long, white arms, the drug reacting, reacting to the drug.

I mean call me Small Town if you like but what sort of background to people come from that enables them to stuff two hundred clams a week up their noses? I mean how stressful can it be being so rich?

Ben hands over the tube and Rob snorts up half of the remaining line and feels an instant tingle.

'Pro-active!' Ben suddenly bursts out, throwing an arm around his shoulder, 'Pro-active!'

Rob stands smiling but not really understanding, stepping towards the door, followed by them.

'Lovely to see you!'

Anything produced under the influence of gear is false, false, false, even smiles.

In the plush hallway he passes an old lady with a plastic countenance, being led along by a nervous poodle on a red leash, opens the main door to let her pass and then realises she's probably had a face-lift – the woman, not the dog.

'How charming, thank you *very* much,'

That bird last night. No doubt she looked like Miss World, thanks to the E but more like she had a face like a dog's bum with a hat on. I was well in and just about to sort the boss with some E's when the Old Bill tips up, come to lecture the boss. 'Drug abuse and how to recognise it' was the lesson. I know the Boss. Nice enough bloke but bent as a U-Bend. The cops tell him what to look out for.

'I'll keep me eyes peeled' he promises, serious.

Cross to the sunny side of the street.

An ecstasy sweat is due. Fucks you right up .The human body's naive: it trusts, it takes everything you offer. When will it fail you? Will it ever?

'Where to, boss?' asks Ahmed.

'Camden Town'

As the automatic slides forward, he glimpses a dusty black man with an Afro, purple shirt and orange trousers, fishing in a green skip full of rubbish.

What use is a life with no destination, wandering aimlessly, nowhere to go when the sun goes down?

He lights a cigarette and smoke wreaths around him as the car chugs through London.

III

The shop fronts and interiors of restaurants and cafes, all modelled on stereotypical designs from all the connected pit stops of the Global Village, mill with diners and drinkers all chasing the elusive spirit of the proverbial 'good time', a spirit that never rests, never settles and probably doesn't even exist. Waiters and potboys balance trays, plates and glasses and weave between the tables and chairs. Humanity is a field, children everywhere, dodging and dreading the forest of adult legs.

The smoke of burning incense dances with the aromas of foods, pubs spill out smoke and the sweet smell of alcohol courts the perfume of carbon monoxide. Leaflets advertising new religions, vegetarian restaurants, craft fairs and gigs are pushed into empty hands and fall to the ground like large fat leaves. Buskers strum Lennon and McCartney or blow freeform into saxophones. Chip wrappers and discarded boxes of half-eaten fried chicken and strips of pizza crust from burger bars forlornly wait for the beggars and dogs to polish them off or the soles of shoes to squash them along the pavement, while madmen with burning eyes and a bed at the Sally Bash lurch leeward, mumbling lost prayers into cans of treacle-strength lager, cursing at European hippies loitering on the bridges, plaiting tourist hair with brightly coloured strings.

First time out of your safe Munich sty is it, Helga? Oh, you are a rebel aren't you, mit your rainbow designer Bennetton shit cloth stupid backpack stuffed mit your fucked up girlie fashions und your fuckink travellers cheques. Sporting a red string in your locks und letting it curl across your Kurt Cobain t-shirt. Oo yes, vat ein fuckink rebel. Stick this up your Kraut hooter unt shutzen-zi uppen.

Reggae plays from ghetto blasters at unlicensed stalls using the tarmac to lay out plastic-coated posters of Bob Marley and maps of Jamaica. African men whisper 'Hashish!' or 'Trips!' from the corners of their unmoving mouths.

Rob takes off his jacket, tosses it over one shoulder and goes down to the Lock where the dank green water of the lower level bubbles like a pot of simmering soup as a barge begins its lazy descent from the upper lock where a man in his shirt-sleeves winds the ratchet that opens the gates.

On the opposite bank a group of girls laugh, shout and dance as a group of guys set up an infectious rhythm of drums. Tourists gather and gawp with their cameras, stealing images. Travellers with long, matted hair and ill-fitting, brightly coloured clothes weave around, happy but dirty mongrels snapping at their heels. The police presence pretends omniscience, looking but not seeing. Strolling on under the bridge where another busker sits cross-legged on the towpath strumming an electric guitar and playing with the fuzz and echo, he throws a handful of change onto the busker's coat. Rob's mobile rings and he fishes it out of his jacket as a black man, in his hands a cradle hanging from straps and inside a tiny white gurgling baby clutching the air with fists like pink tulips.

'Yeah?'

'Is that you?'

'Maybe. Who's this?'

'Bob'

'Bob who?'

'Bob from Fear of Music? Listen, I'm looking to get sorted on a couple of G's of C.'

Fear of Music - party scene awash with people that want to forget reality, dance, bother no one, but some Eton-educated twat will get a law together and shaft us all. Where there is a drive for freedom there is also always a drive for restriction. Who said that? It looks like I just did. Bob? Smoke machines, UV, throbbing one-forty bee pee em, loud, loud, loud. Bob?

'Camden High Street, called Claudio's, hundred yards up from the Tube, half an 'our?'

'Great!'

' 'ow do, Rob, 'ow's things?'

Scouse Fuzzy - African father, Scouse mother - peddles up and circles Rob, slowly pushing the bike around with his feet.

'Know anyone wants to buy a bike?'

'Where'd you nick it?'

'Regent's Park. Some dozy sod left it standing. I thought, 'Aye, aye, I'm having that!' Fifty to you.'

'No thanks,'

'Twenty?'

Shakes his head.

'An E. You can have it for an E!'

Looks at his watch.

'Knock-off credit cards?'

'I'll see you around, Fuzzy.'

'If you need anything, gizza shout!'

Suddenly close by, a scream. In the centre of the canal is an island straddled by two lock gates – one working, the other defunct and rusted shut and the water surface area clogged with floating debris. A stoned body misjudges and slips, disappearing feet-first beneath the surface and popping up a second later, coughing and covered in garbage as hands pull it dripping onto the lock. Fuzzy laughs: 'Fucking hell, I thought I was out of it!' then he pushes down on his pedals and disappears behind a tall, bra-less blonde, platform shoes, shoulder length hair. The mobile rings.

'It's me, it's Alex. You in my neck of the woods, Rob?'

'Keep talking,'

'Come to my place. I've two tarts flying and begging to do a Lesbo show, man! You can have a ring-side!'

Rob waves a cab and climbs in.

'Archway, mate!'

The interior stinks of perfume hiding a deeper odour.

'Sorry abaht the whiff, mate. Some git puked in 'ere last night!'

The cab shunts through the Saturday traffic, grabbing urgently at spaces.

'You can't live your life like it's one long party! You have to be serious some time!'

'But what else is there?'

The jam loosens, allowing the cab to race into Upper Holloway, pushing him back into his seat as they slide past the hairdressers', the toyshop, the record store and the pub on the tree-lined terrace where she lived.

Does she ever think about what we should have said instead of what we did say? I rehearse them like lines in a film, bounce them off images of her in my head so they come back to me as words I can work with – like the happy ending. 'Stop takings drugs!' she screamed, 'You're turning into a fucking zombie!' Study - that's what she decided she was going to do: go straight and study at some college.

IV

The cab stops. He gets out and passes the driver a ten saying: 'Keep the change' then makes for the red door and rings the bell. The door opens, Alex's face a sea of relief, he ushers Rob into the front room. A house-tune on white label plays.

'Where're the birds?'

'Ah, they had to leave, sorry about that. You got me some toot?'

Want to speak out, object, say something, anything, but instead reflect how I allowed myself to be taken in. That was different from just being taken in.

Alex's story: an old man in banking, bought the house for his 21st, stuck him in it and said: 'Get a life!' Now Alex dreams of being a deejay hanging out with the jet-set but is a twenty-one year-old drug fiend, ancient before his time. No discipline.

'What was it you wanted?'

'Just the one,'

Alex hands over some crumpled notes and Rob doesn't even have to count them - he just knows. Alex starts to talk about what he did last night.

But there's nothing more boring than a fool trying to describe the head-state he got himself into in his last session. As if you're bothered. When you choose to take drugs you don't watch from outside, you want to be on the inside looking out. That's why drugs are selfish.

'You're a few quid short, Alex'

'There's eighty there'

'Alex, don't be boring. You owe me a hundred and twenty already - plus sixty for this? That's one hundred and eighty. This is eighty, not a hundred and eighty.'

'Look' says Alex, desperation creeping into his voice, 'I've got a support slot at The Limelight next week supporting Sasha, I'll get you on the Guest List if you like.'

'You're pulling my dick, you couldn't even get on a fucking shopping list!'

'What about a half then? That's thirty and fifty I owe?'

'I don't do halves'

Alex shrugs, defeated.

'Well, you got me, man. All I got's this puff'

He holds out an open square of newspaper with some dried green leaves and sticks.

'So why don't you just smoke it and chill and give yourself a break?'

Alex slumps into the battered sofa.

'Because it's fucking Saturday!' he hisses.

As the stylus jams on the disc, a noise like a pistol shot cracks out over and over.

'Look, I'll leave you a couple of lines and you keep thirty, okay?'

'Aw, brilliant, man! Cheers!'

Rob takes the fifty and leaves three tens on the stereo next to the turntable. He tips out a little of the powder onto a CD case then takes a couple of steps towards the door. Alex is so busy rolling up one of the tens into a tight tube he doesn't even see him leave.

Out in the sunlight two boys play Kerby with a ball and two little girls run around a toy pushchair. He looks in both directions and knows that all roads go somewhere in this city and where there's a road there's always a cab. The mobile rings.

'Where you at? It's Bob! Where are you, man? I thought we were meeting at Claudio's?'

He looks at his watch.

'Down there in ten'

'Two g's, yeah?'

The 'phone clicks off.

I'm not programmed to deal with aliens invading my body. I've no antidotes, no remedies to LSD or E. Brains are like eggs – you can only fry them once.

He suddenly retches but it's like acid and one massive muscle rips his insides from top to bottom like a hunting knife and it makes him double over in agony. The kids stop playing and look. It's not the puking that shocks him - it's just the suddenness of its arrival.

V

'Buenos dias. Tequila?'

'Large whisky please, and a Bud'

Claudio's is hot with the steam of and smells of a busy kitchen, restaurant and bar.

Claudio's is old, if five years is old in the ephemera of Camden, betwixt burger bar and shoe shop. Furniture's superficial - you can gut the place in five minutes, MFI. I know faces and they know me. I got a tab, they let me stay late, cash me cheques sometimes, and staff are nice people – French, Italian, Spanish, models mostly - can't pour a pint for shit, but they look great. Janie's working – she's pretty, twenty-four, twenty-five? Her boyfriend drums in a rock band. What are they called again?

'Hi!' Janie calls, walking to the kitchen with a tray of dirty plates. She drops them off at the hatch and taps her nose.

'Gordon's looking for you,'

Carlos brings over the squat glass of whisky on a small paper serviette. Rob pours down a few mouthfuls and feels his stomach burn. Carlos pushes over a tall, thin bottle of soft, cold beer and gulps down a few mouthfuls.

Feeling a claw-like hand on his shoulder he knows its Gordon.

'See that bird over there?'

A black-as-coal woman sits alone, delicately cutting food in a manner disproportionate to her size.

'Yer genuine Madame, wants to get sumpen sorted for a trick, short notice, doon at The Dorchester. Breaken a new girl in, Roedean or some fucking place.'

A telephone rings and Gordon goes to answer it. As he leaves, he taps his nose and points to the Gents. Rob brushes slips down the corridor behind the kitchen, turning left at the end for the toilet. It's empty. He stands at the urinal and pretends to pee. Seconds later Gordon comes in and together they squeeze into the sole cubicle, locking the door with the small catch. He lays out a line on the plastic cistern.

'On the house,'

'Yer a pal!'

Gordon sniffs it up.

The hinges of the door that connects the Gents to the corridor suddenly creak. Gordon puts a finger to his own lips, but his Glaswegian patience is short and he suddenly bursts out: 'Aw, fook this! Ah'm not frightened getting' caught in me own fookin' restaurant!' and then unlocks the door and crashes out.

'Coast's clear!' he shouts as he leaves. 'I'll send the Madame!'

Rob locks the cubicle door again. Just then the door to the Gents opens again. The cubicle door is pushed. A deep rich voice says: 'Is that Rob?'

'No, it's Mick. Who the fuck's that?'

'Sorry' comes the reply and the Gents door bangs shut again. Rob unlocks the bolt and pops his head out. As he does so, blinking, the door opens again. Madame glances into the tiny space to ensure it's empty and then steps into the cubicle. Wordlessly, she takes his stash from the cistern, peers into the plastic bag and her eyes flicker as she notices some of the wraps are pink and some red. She takes one of each colour. He takes the red and puts it back in the bag.

'Eighty'

'Daylight robbery' she scolds, counting eight tens from a wad of a hundred hiding in her palm.

He smiles as she slips out of the cubicle, counts to ten and then follows her out and back into the restaurant. He retakes his seat and glances across at the Madame who is now re-seated at her table. She looks up at him, through him, back to her plate. He looks away and sucks at the neck of his bottle, glances around for signs of Gordon but there are none. Even Janie has disappeared. He finishes his bottle and asks Carlos for the bill. Carlos taps his nose and says: 'On the house!'

Rob leaves Claudio's and steps out into the street, looking up and down the now pedestrian-heavy pavement. Cars, vans, cabs, buses shunt through the one-way system, nosing slowly towards the buzzing market where impossible crowds swallow them up. He glimpses Fuzzy weaving in and out of the traffic on his stolen mountain bike.

I had a friend once, lived near Tottenham. Been at Broadwater in '85 - wrong place, wrong time. He hadn't killed anyone, no coppers or nothing. Just petty thieving: kettles, videos and cameras. Old Bill picks him up and bangs him away for three days. Then they make him an offer he can't refuse: grass everyone you've ever met in your life ever that's ever done the slightest bent thing and you walk. So he did, even down to people he smoked with. I got tipped off they were coming so I packed me few bits and checked out. I wasn't what I am now. Back then I was a drifter, just shipped in from up north. Making friends, smoking dope, running cons, neither thief nor dealer. I took everything that was offered me, just like me Mum and Dad. And look at them: waiting to die like a Nazi gag at a UB40 concert. Okay, Bob, you missed your chance.

The mobile rings.

'It's Jeremy. Where are ya?'

Jeremy: decent bloke, touch more fond of the bottle than the powder, bit paranoid, journo for The Guardian - mid-forties, Blackpool.

'Got about a dozen people 'ere in t'garden. They're not poor. Loads of food, loads of booze but not much else.'

VI

Jazz feeds from speakers placed out in the sun. Sausages and burgers sizzle over a charcoal fire at one end of the garden, the air blue with smoke. Names come and go. Jeremy takes Rob by the arm and steers him towards the kitchen.

'I just got back from South America. Commissioned to do a write-up on the rainforest. Good money in timber. Half the Habitats in Europe are stuffed with it, allegedly. I met a lot of wankers, shook loads of hands, did a lot of talking, mountains of paperwork, interviews, notes and R and D, but no energy to put it all together you know?'

Robs sucks on his beer, leaning back against the fridge freezer, looks around, antiques, statuettes, rugs, vases, books, PC, mirrors, plants. Jeremy takes out two cigarettes from a packet, lighting them both with a silver Zippo.

'Pal of mine from German Embassy knows where he can score some good coke, right? Two dollars a gram! Two fucking dollars!'

Rob unwraps his stash and places two pinks on the kitchen worktop. Jeremy unfolds one of them and starts chopping it with a fish knife.

'So we pool our bread and I stop outside this hotel while Hans, that's me German mate, goes in and scores. He comes out with a big brown paper bag full off something. I'm thinking it must be a bag of weed or summat, it's so fuckin' big. We get back to the hotel and I say, 'How much you get then?' and he says it's the whole bag! There must have been a fucking kilo there man! This gear would have pulled ten grand on the streets of London! Anyway, I spent the rest of me time out of fucking tree, garbling non-stop into me Dictaphone. The editor says it's the most comprehensive piece I've ever written - daft cunt.'

Jeremy's straw moves quickly along the shaving mirror.

'Mine must be a bit of a let down after Peru,'

'Aye, well, beggars can't be choosers. I'll get the others,' he says, wiping his nose on the back of his hand and going off towards the garden. Slowly but surely a procession of guests are shepherded across to move their noses along lines cut for them. Smiles. Greetings. Thanks.

One girl laughs and puts her hand on her chest as if to protect herself from her own ignorance.

'What do I do?'

Jeremy gives her the straw.

'Now, stick one end just into your left nostril, press your other nostril then move along the line sucking it up through the straw.'

Jeremy winks at me as the woman labours along the line. She lets out a little cry and grimaces as if going to sneeze.

'What happens?'

'You get high, Gwen, you get high!'

'Oh' she laughs nervously, 'fine. Okay then. I'll go and do that!'

'Fucks like a rabbit that one!' says Jeremy as Gwen departs.

'Is that the lot? There's still a bit left.'

'There's Josie? I'll go and get her.'

Jeremy does a double take.

'And mind: Josie's my leg over tonight!'

He goes out into the garden. The crowd is louder now, more animated. Voices pitch drunkenly, punctuated by erratic laughter. Jeremy re-appears with Josie. Josie and Rob look at each other.

It's funny isn't it, when you just know you're going to get your end away?

She picks up the straw and snorts up her line like a veteran then leans back against the kitchen table, doing a little pirouette on her knuckles.

'Nothing to write home about. San Diego, if you're thinking of asking. My Dad's American. You do E's?'

'Yes'

'What are they?'

'Does it matter?'

'Are they good?'

'You want one?'

'How much?'

'You can afford it'

'I guess'

Jeremy re-appears with a dinner plate, on which are scattered notes and coins.

'You like the coke, Josie?'

'Rob and I were thinking of splitting, going over to my place in Islington.'

'So soon?' Jeremy queries, troubled.

'I'll go and get my jacket,' she says.

As Josie disappears, Jeremy turns and pokes a finger into his shoulder.

'Thanks a fucking bunch!'

'No big deal. I give her the E, she gives me the bread, and I split.'

'I bet that's not all you'll be giving her! I've brought your money.'

Jeremy opens his cupped palms and silver, copper and paper slides onto the fridge top.

'What is this, a collection plate?'

'You're getting the ride for nowt!'

Rob quickly calculates.

'That's only a ton. Don't fuck me, J!'

'I'm not fucking *you*!'

What the fuck good ever came out of Blackpool anyway?

Josie re-appears, black Ray-Bans across her face, a crumbling spliff hanging from her lips. She puts on her red jacket, sucks in a lungful of smoke and passes it to Jeremy.

'Thanks. Great bar-b, J. See you next time!'

'Aye. Next time. Pop back later if you want. We're all going down the pub.'

Josie kisses Jeremy on the cheek and lies: 'Yeah, sure'

Rob throws his jacket over his shoulder and he and Josie walk out to find a cab.

VII

He looks at her as she gazes from the window. One leg
rocks gently across the other as the cab takes the bumps.
The mobile rings. Josie looks at him and then back from
the window.

'Fuck's going on man? Supposed to be meeting you at
Claudio's! Been waiting an hour!'

'What's your number?'

'Where are you now?'

'Tied up. What's your number?'

'Tell me where,'

Josie's hand reaches his leg and squeezes it. She looks at
him, seeking the same reassuring eye contact as when
they first met in Jeremy's kitchen.

'I'll call you back,'

'Another customer?' Josie asks.

The mobile rings.

'Bob, will you -!' starts Rob.

'This is the voice of your conscience calling'

'Alana?'

'Hello'

I call him by the name he chooses: Alana - but Alana is really Alan. Rents a flat near King's Cross Looks like a woman, dresses, makes-up, walks, sits, fucks like a woman. Lives in a woman's space, clean, immaculate, fresh, a bunch of flowers in a vase on a coffee table. 'Beautiful TV – Realise Your Dreams' as the cards say. City types bossing their secretaries by day, wanked off in stockings and sussies by Alana at night. Alana is saving up for the snip. We're in the same sort of line of business in a way: relaxation. Alana always pays in full too, no credit.

'Will you be able to stop by about seven?'

'Seven'

'Thanks, darling'

The line goes dead.

'Girlfriend?' asks Josie.

Alison called me a megalomaniac once. I had to look it up in the dictionary. 'You're turning into a fucking megalomaniac!' she shouts. 'What the fuck is that?' I shouts back, her sobbing down the 'phone line at me in Hampstead. 'I'm going straight, I swear!' but even as I say it I'm cradling the 'phone between chin and shoulder, cutting up lines and otherwise raving with half a dozen other losers about grandiose plans to open an Amsterdam-type coffee shop in Notting Hill. What a twat eh? And not just Ally but all those that tried, try, will try to help me. I've been called ten types of cunt in my life but never that M word. That M word really stuck. So we split up and the customary binges followed. I first chatted Ally up in a paddy bar. Some wanker said she was born with a mattress on her back but I didn't care. I loved her from the first moment. She told me after that same wanker had tried to shag her she'd fucked him off 'cause the rumour was he'd AIDS, so she asked him for twenty quid cab fare and from then on he went 'round telling everyone she was a slag. First night out we done a couple of trips, stared at the full moon and then I fucked her up the arse. Is that love? Fucking a girl you love up the arse? Is that all there is to it?

Josie coughs. She holds an open box of cigarettes. He takes one, she takes one and lights both.

'What are you thinking about?' she asks.

'Nothing,'

'No smoking please!' the driver calls back.

They salvage deep drags and Rob throws his from the window in a flurry of sparks and Josie nips the end of hers and puts it back in the box. The cab pulls up at a large terraced house just off Islington High Street - spiked railings, Georgian façade, basement steps and Venetian blinds jealously coveting the interior from the exterior world. Josie gets out first.

'You are coming in?'

He hesitates and then gets out and pays the driver. Josie fiddles with some keys and opens the door. He follows, feeling soft carpet under his boots. An odd silence envelops them. The hallway goes down to an open door to what looks like a kitchen beyond. A reedy, upper class voice croaks: 'Josie? Is that you, darling?'

'My Mom' Josie says.

An older version of Josie appears, her head framed around the doorway, and sees him. She is smartly dressed and heavily made up despite the incongruity of the pink apron and green rubber gloves.

What sort of bird puts her make-up on to do the washing?

'Would your friend like coffee or tea?'

'Neither, thank you'

'Something stronger?' asks Josie. 'Daddy's an alcoholic.'

And I hate grown people who still call their folks Mummy and Daddy.

The mobile rings. He reaches into his pocket, takes it out and switches it off and turns to ask Josie for the money, but she's halfway up the stairs.

'The money's in my room' she calls down, disappearing at the top.

He follows, whispering Josie's name. He sees a door at the top, half open. Beyond is a full-length mirror on the wall and he sees Josie pull her shirt from her shoulders, reach around and unhook her bra and then push her white knickers over her hips and kick them off her ankles. He climbs the last few steps and goes into the room. Josie is laid back on a bed, naked. Her body is young and firm with unblemished skin and a tuft of short, black, curly hair between her legs, her breasts hanging on her ribs have body to them and he knows instantly he'd like to touch, weigh, knead them. But that's all. He knows that raising the dead would be easier than raising an erection. Josie is holding a remote. A video clicks into life. The image flickers: an old man with a young woman laid face down across his lap. The old man gloats at the woman's defencelessness, rubbing bony hands over her backside. The camera wobbles in and out of focus as the old man starts slapping his palm firmly on alternate cheeks of the woman's backside. Josie reaches out and unbuckles Rob's belt. Her fingers slip inside and squash his flaccid prick. He sits down next to her on the bed and watches the screen as she wanks him. He allows her to pull him a few times but then he jumps to his feet and fastens his pants.

'What's wrong?'

'I'd like to squeeze your tits.'

'Squeeze them then' she says, looking down at each of her breasts.

He gets down on his knees and reaches out. Josie closes her eyes and reacts like electricity. His fingers and palms squash and squeeze her small breasts. He is hypnotised by the sight and the feeling. There is a knock at the door.

'Josie? I've brought you some juice.'

He stands.

'Wait!' whispers Josie.

He waits – two, three, four, five. He opens the bedroom door. A tray of Robinson's Barley Water, two glasses and a jug of water on a tray are on the carpet.

'I'm going,' he says.

'Stay,' says Josie.

He fastens his pants and steps over the tray of juice and descends the stairs quickly and lets himself out of the house. Within a minute he's rejoined the shoppers and tourists strolling in the sun on the High Street. He waves a cab. Activating his mobile again, he asks the cabbie if it's okay to smoke and when the reply is positive he lights up.

'Camden Town, please mate!'

VIII

'Situation is I've just had a call from one of my clients. He's stocked up on green and hard but wants a few g's and party tickets.'

'How much is a few, Joe?'

'Three G's and thirty tickets?'

'Six hundred'

'You gotta give me a discount!'

'I'm giving you a discount, Joe'

'Thirty quid? Come on!'

'Yes or no?'

'I'm lodging an official protest to the Dealers Union here, mate. Where are you?'

'King's Cross'

'Come down Cambridge Circus then call me again'

The mobile rings again.

' 'ello, mate!'

'George, what's up?'

' 'ow'd them E's go down larst night?'

'Like nectar'

' 'ow many'd you do?'

'A couple,'

'A couple? Kamikaze's the right fackin' name for 'em, I tell you. Listen, I got a rave out near Milton Keynes tonight. I was wondering if you could pop by my gaff and sort me say seven g's? I'd appreciate it.'

'No probs. Listen, I'm glad you rang. Do you know a face called Bob Sharp?'

' 'oo?'

'Bob Sharp'

'Maybe. I know lots of faces but no names. What's 'e look like?'

'Good point, don't know.'

'Well, watch your back. I'll think on it. See you about eight, okay?'

He leans forward and calls to the cabbie: 'Change of plan, mate, Cambridge Circus'

'Right, guv!'

First off: Soho, to sort three to Mobile Joe and net five big ones. I'll need a G for Alana and George wants seven. I've twenty more ready-to-go at home and another twenty's worth uncut in the cupboard. I've only five on me so I'm gonna have to go back anyway to sort out what I'm packing tonight. Then of course I've got to shoot over to Battersea and pick up that big order for Andy. It's going to be a busy and lucrative night.

He taps Karen's number into the mobile.

'Karen?'

First met Karen at a rave - where else? - friend of Gordon's. 'What you on?' she says. 'What you got?' I say. She gave me a scented spliff and I toked on it. Fuck me, I reeled. Legs turned to fucking jelly.

'What the fuck is that?'

'They call it keif. It's from Morocco!'

Then the younger girl behind her took the spliff.

'This is my daughter, Karen.'

It was a full house that night. John Digweed was playing. Karen pulls me into a corner and hands me a straw and a snuffbox full of toot and gives me a blast - nine out of ten.

I met them again New Year's Eve, both E'd to the gills. I give the daughter one from behind in the Gents over a pan blocked with shit and bog roll. It wasn't genuine attraction just that illusion E gives that everyone is beautiful when you know fine well everyone's pig ugly. Gillian wants a relationship but it's a bad move, fucking your dealer's only daughter.

The cab gallops down the Gower Street one-way system, three vehicles abreast and fifty deep, roaring like cavalry towards Bloomsbury, cruising through amber-to-red, scuffing up purple smog.

'Are you still there?'

'Yeah, yeah'

'If you want them all weighed and bagged individually I can get Billy to do it but it'll take a while and I'll have to slap another ton on for the time.'

'Loose is fine, Karen.'

'What's your schedule?' (he noted she pronounced 'sch' as a k)

'I can be there between eight and nine?'

'Bit more specific?'

'Eight-thirty?'

'See you then, pet.'

The cab pulls up at one end of Shaftsbury Avenue. Rob gets out, pays the driver, produces the mobile and calls Mobile Joe. In the background Rob can hear tinny pop music playing.

'Old Compton Street - first block on the left to the right of The Spice of Life. There's a red neon sign sticking out. See it?'

He glances along the road and sees LIVE BED SHOW in neon red.

'I'm holding the fort for a mate of mine. Come up the stairs.'

Rob finds himself climbing dirty stairs. An old man with a scared face descends and they pass halfway. At the top a blue curtain hangs. He moves it aside. He can hear that tinny pop music again. A bare bulb is the only light. A tart sits behind a red Formica table smoking a cigarette.

'Ten pounds for the show'

'I'm looking for Joe'

The tart looks him up and down and then disappears behind the bead curtain and calls Joe's name. Joe's face appears.

'Thank fuck, man! I'm petrified Old Bill coming in. Come through.'

He follows Joe into a small room. Joe sits on the edge of a table. He wears black jeans and white training shoes. Thick, black curly hair tumbles over his t-shirted shoulders, eyes concealed by mirror shades. There's an unplugged telephone on the table and a polystyrene cup half-full of a brown liquid in which cigarette ends have been extinguished. In one of the walls there is a small square window from which a purple light shines.

'Sorry about this dump' Joe apologises.

He puts his nose to the small window. A purple bulb shines down on a many-sided room. Each of the walls that make up the many sides has a letterbox-like slot cut into it about two thirds of the way from the floor. On the floor, in the centre of this space, a large, bored woman wearing a see-through purple leotard peddles an exercise bike, a lit cigarette dangling from her lips. He turns back to Joe as Joe pulls a wad from his jeans and counts out some notes.

'Four-fifty you said wasn't it?'

'Five,'

'I'll never be fucking rich at this rate,' Joe grumbles.

'What's new anyway?'

'Not much. Just had a run-in with a septic who's fond of E's and S & M'

'Yeah? Should send her down here, better than these old slags. We'll have to have a session on the pool again you and me. Revenge match.'

Rob counts out three pinks and thirty ecstasy pills on the table. Joe counts out five hundred pounds in a variety of denominations.

'Any time, mate, anytime.'

He unwraps a red, rolls one of the tens up into a tight tube, snorts a little from the packet and then offers Joe the tube.

'Don't say I never give you nothing!'

'Cheers, mate!'

Joe snorts up a little from the wrap. Then he goes to the window and says: 'Fucking state of this!'

'Nice shades. Let's have a look.'

Absently, Joe takes them off and passes them over.

That's all I wanted to know.

'You doing the fucking skag again innit?'

Joe grabs the shades and puts them back on.

'Fuck you. You can't lecture me.'

And he's right of course. I can't.

'So, how about that game then? Say tomorrow night? Down the Hall? About ten?'

'Why not?'

'Don't be late!'

Giving Joe's palm a quick slap and gathering up the money from the table, Rob turns and trots back down the stairs and into the street. Across the road a few people sit in a coffee bar, tables and chairs on the pavement, cool, chic, trendy.

Picture this: Putney, nineteen eighty-eight. Six kids injecting themselves with junk one night. Next morning only five kids wake up. Poor Baz - rigor mortis in his armchair. Of course we rifled his pockets, took his money, his dope, before calling the ambulance. Poor medic. Sunday morning it was. He could have been laid in bed or spending time with his wife and kids but instead he was here in some shitty bed-sit with five junkie fucks. What a funeral: family tossing flowers on his coffin and junkie mates tossing wraps of gear for his journey to the next world.

The cab journey is slow with heavy Saturday evening traffic, Tottenham Court Road, Euston Tower, Mornington Crescent. The mobile rings.

'It's Bob! Now what's going on?'

'Where are you?'

'Wardour Street. You?'

'I thought you was supposed to be waiting for me in Camden?'

'Where can we hook up then?'

This fucking drug life. Pumping shit in, pissing it out, in, out, backwards and forwards, up and down.

IX

Shelves of sunlight slide in and stretch out the dust as he opens the blinds. A CD in the Kenwood pushes out a gentle, easy sound of ambient synthesisers and here and there smoked joints, unused papers, scattered CD's and cases, empty wine bottles, dirty socks, papers unread and shiny porno.

In his bedroom he pulls out a shoebox from the bottom of the wardrobe, takes out the cash from his pockets and drops it on the carpet alongside the takings from the night before. He reckons there's about fifteen hundred but doesn't count. He plugs in his mobile to re-charge it then lights a cigarette and goes through to the bathroom to run a hot bath.

He smokes his cigarette and then puts it out and rolls and smokes half a grass joint by the time the bath is full. So he turns off the taps, undresses and lies back in the water.

I don't dream much anymore because of drugs. But my perfect dream, my manipulated daydream, is a room full of film and rock stars, sitting in an exclusive bar some place hot. One by one they come across to my table and shake hands, hidden within their hands are Gold Cards and notes. I smile at them and they smile at me. We exchange inane bollocks and then shake again in parting, passing to them a variety of concealed drugs. Then Brigitte Nielsen appears. Those fucking legs man! She strides towards a door and beckons me to follow with a crafty wink. I go to the door and push but it's locked. So I laugh nervously and knock. No answer. I keep knocking. Knocking.

Robs opens his eyes, blinks and then struggles to his feet, water pouring from his body onto the carpet as he steps into the hallway and listens. He tiptoes naked and dripping to the stereo, turns down the volume then back to the front door and looks through the spy hole. The fish-eye view shows an Oriental face that he's never seen before. It has shiny, straight black shoulder-length hair and a light grey suit. The stranger looks at his wristwatch, steps back and up at the house and then turns and walks back out to the road.

Back in his bathroom, Rob finds a towel and dries himself down. He wanders out to the patio. The lawn is neat, framed on three sides by flowerbeds. There is no back gate. The only entrance and exit is through the front door. A gentle breeze hushes in the conifers and a fat cat sits on a wall and bees hop from flower to flower. He looks at his watch and then returns to his bedroom where he dresses and stocks up with the twenty pre-prepared bags of cocaine, a hundred pounds in cash, his denim jacket and mobile 'phone. Finally, he takes out ten grand in two rolls of a hundred fifties tied tightly with elastic bands. One goes in each boot, each having a small strip of leather deliberately stitched in a few months earlier by a Camden cobbler.

I've drugs, I've cash and I've a mission. A man needs a mission.

X

'Alana, sorry I'm late - traffic.'

Rob perches on the edge of a turquoise two-seater in front of a glass-topped coffee table.

'Someone's in a hurry,' Alana says, sitting herself down opposite. 'Would you like a glass of something?'

'What have you got?'

'Let me surprise you'

Alana, having poured his long, masculine legs into black stockings that fall from a tight mini skirt, stands and totters to the kitchenette. Around his non-existent breasts is a strapless, red Lycra top and his curly Afro is moulded into a glossy meringue. He returns with two flutes of white wine that catch the sun and wink like prisms.

'Coteaux du Layon - it's French. The chap in the wine shop insists on giving me an education.'

'What was it you wanted again?'

'One, for personal,'

Rob brings out a red wrap and puts it on the coffee table. Alana pushes a fifty, a twenty and a ten back across then goes to a bookcase and from behind one of the half dozen or so books brings a straw, a credit card and a small round mirror. Tipping a little coke onto the mirror and chopping two small lines, Alana snorts up the first and offers the other to Rob. He doesn't object, snorting up the coke and feeling it fall quickly into his throat. He finds himself staring at Alana's legs.

'Oh God, is there a mark? Scotsmen. I don't need bruises. I've a client arriving any minute. He's very punctual. If you ever need me, you know I'm here.'

What on earth have you got that I could possibly need?

XI

George showed me a photo of himself once, many moons ago: shaved head, skin-tights, Doc Martens, about sixteen, seventeen. Told me about his exploits. How he'd met Natalie, his wife, in a riot at Brixton throwing bricks and bottles at the police. They'd both been wearing masks but had still fallen in love.

'We didn't jus' go to riot. We went to lodge a protest – albeit wiv a brick. Got caught in a runnin' battle, so she hid me in Brixton 'ill. Destiny, mate, destiny.'

George has grown his hair back with a vengeance. It's blond, thick, wavy and waist-length. Natalie is short and round with long black hair and coffee-coloured skin. Their six year-old, Maddy, opens the front door. She wears a pink dress and has her brown hair plaited in two pigtails tied with red ribbon. She sticks two fingers into her mouth and says: 'Daddy's looking for you!'

George is at the cooker in the kitchen. The smell of spices fills the air as he stirs something in a wok.

' 'ello mate 'ow's it goin'?' says George looking up. He wipes his hands on his jeans and shakes hands.

Natalie comes from the garden and kisses him on the cheek. There is a little scream followed by another and then a young voice shouts: 'Don't do that or I'll tell!'

Maddy and a young friend skitter into the kitchen. Natalie gently scolds them and ushers them into the garden.

'I put that curry powder in like you told me to, Nat, but its still runny-lookin', '

'Then you didn't put enough in,' says Natalie in her gentle singsong Anglo-Indian lilt, spooning some more onto the dish.

'Bit 'ot for a curry innit?'

'We eat ice cream in winter an' curry in summer. What can I say? Let's go upstairs.'

As George walks to the foot of the stairs and Rob gets up to follow, Natalie asks: 'You are staying for some food?'

'Just eaten, Nat,' he lies. 'Smells great though!'

He follows George up the stairs. At the top, George stands waiting in his bedroom, the top drawer of a chest open, rummaging inside. Rob goes in and sits on the edge of the unmade bed and savours the scent of slumber. A crayon drawing of a smiling face with long yellow hair and another face with long black straight hair is framed and mounted on the wall above the bed. He notices the rag doll pinned to the floor under George's foot.

'Them Kamikaze's 'ave been goin' down a storm at Dance Inevitable,' says George.

Rob holds a thick sheaf of notes. Dampening the tip of his finger he counts out the money for George and then takes out the stash from his jacket.

'You tooled up?'

'Tooled up?'

'I tell you for why I ask - I was comin' aht the George Robey the other day an' some cunt pulled a blade an' demanded money wiv menaces, as the pigs say.'

'You're joking?'

'Naw. Seen it comin' though: by the wrist – head-butt, bosh, taxi 'ome. Not a word to Nat mind. You gotta be prepared, mate, nasty world out there!'

George hands over a wad and puts seven red wraps on the bed. Maddy bursts in.

'What you doin'?'

'Daddy's busy, sweetheart.' George picks her up and tickles her. 'Busy, busy, busy!'

'Busy, busy, busy!' she imitates. He covers the seven red squares with one hand and smiles at her and Maddy calms down and asks her dad: 'Will you ask 'im if he wants to stay for dinner?'

'Why don' you ask 'im yourself?'

'I'm shy!' she says, burying her face in George's shoulder. George winks and gathers up the seven red squares and drops them in the top drawer with the socks. He closes it and strides out to the stairs with Rob following.

'You ain't gonna make much on seven, George?' whispers Rob.

'Can get seventy or eighty a g at this do tonight - middle class yuppies. I'll keep one for personal and knock out the other six at eighty and cream a ton plus profit. All counts. You any idea 'ow much it costs to bring up a kid? They grow so bleedin' fast an' we're savin' to get in this prep school down the road.'

George kisses Maddy on the cheek.

'Stayin' for a bit of grub then?'

Rob shakes his head.

'You wanna look after yourself better. Eat proper. Get yourself a good woman, 'ave some kids. Makes a world of difference. I was a boy 'til I had this 'un.'

They descend the stairs and open the front door. George follows, depositing Maddy at the bottom.

'You ravin' tonight?'

'Yeah. Kerry's took out an office block in Shoreditch someplace.'

'I've 'eard about that. Say hello to 'er for me. You be needin' any more pills?'

'Next weekend prob'ly.'

'Aw'right, mate. Look after yourself and stay lucky!'

They touch fists and he walks down the street, once waving at Maddy.

Kids? What's that all about then? Think the world turns around them. Expensive too. Consuming, demanding, wanting. Giving fuck all back. Love? And what'll they do with you when you're old? Bang you up in a fucking old folks' home is what! Love. How many cans of brew and spliffs can love buy in a city where the only currency is cash? George swatted a fly. My soft spot that. I'd need a shooter to feel truly safe, even if it just fired blanks, even the sight of the fucker'd scare any bastard off. I try to see myself behaving in a certain way, anticipating, reacting wisely, firmly, but at the end of the day I see an ignominious end in a gutter, a pathetic end to a pathetic life. Better to explode in brief glory like a firework rocket than hang in endless space like a burnt out planet. Stay lucky. Life ain't fuck like Hollywood.

Saturday is market day in Portobello. The traders have mostly gone but some shoppers and tourists still string together a dwindling atmosphere in the gathering dew of early evening. Rob stops and looks about - against a wall a few old dresses hang from coat hangers hooked into chips in the wall and blankets lay on the pavement on which an old toothless bag lady has placed a few pairs of shoes. A man with a too-expensive grey summer jacket and black hair inspects a pair of brown brogues. The bag lady addresses him but he doesn't respond. Robs turns and sees he's standing outside a pub. Ranks queue at the bar. He finds the Gents and locks himself in a cubicle then fishes out one of the red squares, rolls a ten-pound note into a tube and snorts. He sniffs hard to get it into his throat then wipes his nose with the back of his hand and exits. Back at the bar he's alert but edgy, scrutinising every movement, sounds amplified. He catches the barman's attention and orders a large scotch – no ice – and a pint of the strongest. The scotch goes down swiftly and the lager follows in gulps. He belches loudly. He is aware of faces staring. He goes out to find a cab.

Yeah, dealing's dangerous but it's not my fault. It's The Berlin Wall see? And what's the alternative for a man with no qualifications in this city? Idiot companies, idiot people, idiot products, idiot wages, shirt and ties, ticked off like a kid, endless, mundane, competition, death, insane, futile, pointless journey. It all hinges on perspectives and interpretations.

XII

Battersea - a once-derelict warehouse that took its trade from the river, now a prime residential location taking its trade from the city and from the street.

Rob leaves the cab and, walking into the cul-de-sac, glances at Karen's block, squatting like a scrubbed brick-sphinx behind a wall tipped with gun-barrel-grey spearhead railings.

Standing at an iron gate between two columns, on the left a camera, he presses a button on the silver panel in the wall and waits. The camera buzzes as it turns and tilts like a condescending butler. Security lights flood upwards from recesses in the manicured gardens that flank the gates. There is an audible but muffled clunk as the mechanism trips a bolt and it silently opens. He steps in and goes up to the door to the block. As he presses another button on another panel, the gates to the street lock behind with a clang and another buzzing follows like the raucous rasp of an amplified wasp so he pushes open the glass door and walks across the marble floor past the tinkling fountain and into the open lift. The doors hiss behind him and it carries him silently up to the top of the three floors where Billy meets him.

Emlyn I call him - like Emlyn Hughes, you know, that funny voice? Billy met Karen when he'd been homeless, roughing it. Legend has it Billy saved Karen from a mugger and she rewarded him by taking him off the streets, giving him a place to live and time to sort his life out. He's been her bodyguard ever since. It could be me - part of the firm. Company car. Free rein. Petrol all paid for. Spare room for overnight stays. Alternate shifts. A basic grand a week plus perks.

No.

No control. Punters, kids, hookers, bankers, pop stars, TV presenters, priests, cops, politicians, moving money around, anonymous-looking pick-ups and drop-offs, backwards and forwards to Amsterdam twice a month, Interpol, Hit Squads, major, major prison sentences.

No, no, no.

Billy/Emlyn comes forward, the Scouse accent incongruous from that wall of muscle, reminding him of an asthmatic schoolgirl.

'Karen says: 'Go in. Sit down. Don' say a word 'til she says. Got it?'

Rob nods but doesn't get it.

Karen is speaking on the telephone, sitting in a plush swivel chair on one side of a desk. On the desk next to her: an ashtray, a packet of cigarettes, a lighter, a glass and half a bottle of gin. She turns and smiles briefly then continues to swivel until he is facing the back of her chair once again.

He sits on an equally comfortable chair on the other side of the desk. A gentle push with his feet and it turns, letting him take in the sheer expanse of the place: huge plate glass windows from ceiling to floor replace at least two walls and, usually, offer panoramic views across London, the Thames and Victoria. But tonight the view is blocked by roller-shutters. Red leather Burgundy armchairs, a king size snooker table with an unfinished game, a thin bookcase bearing the weight of one lone volume, a marble table that would easily double as an altar to a Greek god, a number of other tables piled high with three major computers, two of which functioned, surrounded by banks of CD's, colour printers, keyboards and at least two satellite telephones. Behind, a corridor runs down to where he knows four huge rooms split off. The door directly at the end of the corridor suddenly opens and Gillian, towelling her wet hair, motions for him to come over. He swivels the chair back to face Karen and waits. A minute later, Karen puts the 'phone down and turns and looks at him and smiles. She stands and comes round, leans down and whispers in his ear:

'The room's bugged'

He starts to speak but Karen puts a finger on his lips and whispers: 'I've a friend due.'

He wonders: can they be just seen or just heard or both? Windows enable occupants to see out but could just as easily allow others to see in, though if the apartment was being spied on they'd have to have telescopic lenses, as there were no other windows at the same level close to Karen's block. The door buzzer rings. Karen goes to the door with Billy and presses a button on the VDU. She presses another switch and then, folding her arms tightly about herself, looks down at the carpet, waiting.

I want an ice-cold beer and a line and a spliff and a bottle of Moet & Chandon and an open-topped Thunderbird cruising down the beach road on a cool sunset evening and two naked big-titty bisexual valley girls giving me a BJ. And I do not want to be here right now.

The door opens and a nondescript, balding man with small round spectacles and wearing a grey Mackintosh enters, carrying a briefcase he puts down on the table next to the computer hardware, opening it. He raises his eyebrows and looks at Karen who replies with a question mark on her face. He smiles - evidently they know each other. Taking out a small black box that looks like an old-fashioned tape recorder, he fits the headphones leading from it over his thinning hair and clamps them onto his ears. Producing a hand-held device resembling a TV remote, he begins his sweep.

With Karen's desk and all the computer equipment he is particularly thorough, soon producing as if by a magician's sleight-of-hand a small button-shaped object he holds up to the light bulb to scrutinise like a diamond-engraver. He raises his eyebrows then whispers something to Karen who points to her glass. He drops it into the gin. His sweep moves to the rest of the room: the snooker table, the bookcase and the armchairs. Another is discovered fixed by adhesive to the underside of the bookcase and is soon dropped into the same glass. Then he sweeps the kitchen, followed everywhere by Karen with Billy shadowing. Rob stays in his chair, watching from a comfortable distance, fascinated. Karen taps at the bathroom door and Gillian steps out in fresh clothes as they go in and then re-emerge. After a cursory nose around the edges of the room and the windows, after he removes his headphones and says: 'You're clean', tension drains from the room. Karen lights a cigarette and smoke fans out.

'Thanks, Phil. It's good of you.'

Phil nods and smiles. Karen looks at Billy who hands a brown envelope to Phil. Phil slips it into an inside pocket.

'You can get devices to baffle and confuse but they do cost or you could tint your windows.'

'What would you suggest, Phil?'

'Move,' says Phil with his best effort at a smile.

He shakes Karen's hand, packs away his equipment and leaves without a second glance.

'Retired Detective Sergeant. It pays to have contacts.'
Rob bends down, pulls his jeans up over his left boot, slips his fingers inside and brings out the roll.

'Half a K wasn't it?'

She must be bringing in twenty, thirty, forty grand a week. The mind boggles. It's costing her a packet in pay-offs, but she's still loaded. Of course I'm not the only punter. I'm one of a small army. Down in the basement of the building are garages for the block's three apartments where Karen's jeep and sports car live. Her neighbours are a record producer and a B-rated celebrity. I've never seen her looking so vulnerable then though, chewing her nails, chain-smoking like a single Mum backed into a corner by screaming kids and a punch-drunk husband.

'Who do you reckon?'

Karen peels off her rubber gloves, removes the facemask and produces two glasses. Breaking the seal on a fresh bottle of Jameson's, she pours one for herself and one for Rob. Pressing a switch near the window, the roller-shutters hum up into the ceiling and a stunning golden sunset invades the space, flooding in, drenching the occupants and the décor in a red and yellow haze. She slides the patio doors and a life-saving breeze gently ladles out the thick atmosphere of the room.

'It's easy to get into this business, Rob, but not so easy to get out.'

He feels suddenly uncomfortable, almost embarrassed, standing there leaning against the balcony rail, as this woman who could have passed as a socially-besieged council house Mum, spills out intimate thoughts to him, another dealer, a stranger. They say nothing and then Billy saves the day by appearing with a briefcase.

Rob leaves, a kiss on the cheek being the only memorable event. The cab stops at lights behind Buckingham Palace where two drunks fight and wrestle on the pavement.

In the briefcase is half a kilo of cocaine. It could send me down for seven to ten. Now, I'm not a violent man. I've not murdered anyone directly nor stolen money with menaces and I've never even touched a gun except at a fairground. I've never raped anyone or attempted to murder. And yet for what I carry in my briefcase I can be sent to a place where people that have committed all of the above reside, for seven to ten. Karen kissed me on the cheek, told me to be extra careful, extra vigilant and Billy had scanned with the CCTV. I've got this feeling I'm not going to see her again, for a while. Where does that leave me?

The mobile rings. With half a kilo of cocaine in his briefcase, he knows he shouldn't answer it. He knows he should let it ring or switch it off altogether, get back to Camden and safely stash the case but . . .

Colin, a friend of Alex's from Holloway, wants me to meet him at a pub called The Hare & Hounds near Vauxhall to sell ten E's. The pub runs strippers six nights a week and doubles up as a drug pad, a watering hole near a council estate where dealers ferret through the labyrinthine parks and alleys to quench thirsts and do business. But a man in my position cannot just walk into a pub like The Hare & Hounds, dressed like a fucking cowboy and carrying a briefcase. So I've worked it to meet Col outside, across the street and do the deal via handshakes, quickly and efficiently so the cabbie doesn't suspect.

Given fresh instructions, the cabbie executes a swift U-turn and goes back over Vauxhall Bridge, pulling up, after some tight corners, a few minutes later on the opposite side of The Hare & Hounds. A heartbeat after and two police vans, sirens conspicuously mute, are outside. Their back doors fly open, uniformed DS in flak jackets, vests, helmets and truncheons, spill out and pour into the pub through the front. Two more DS with agitated German Shepherds guarding either side. The interior quietens - and then all hell breaks loose. A gunshot's fired – or something very loud - and a chair crashes through the plate glass window and onto the pavement. A woman screams and the German Shepherds start barking and strain to be loose.

'Get the fuck out!' Rob shouts to the cabbie.

The cabbie doesn't need telling twice. It jerks forward as its wheels thumb the road, execute a swift U-ey, back past the same pub - a woman runs out, cabbie hits the brakes, another bod runs out, grabs the door handle my side, swings it half open. Rob recognises Colin but not

Colin has his eyes elsewhere. Rob grabs the door and slams it shut again and Colin releases under pressure from a cop tackling him from behind.

Though, apart from stopping off once at a late night chemist the journey is otherwise uneventful, Rob cannot take his eyes away from the RV. The driver's eyes glance in it every few seconds, weighing him up, watching like a hawk, knowing something is not quite right about his fare and yet at the same time knowing the fare is honourable as long as he's a passenger.

Back home shortly after, Rob puts on rubber gloves and a facemask and puts his half-key on a table. He opens another fresh plastic bag and using a plastic teaspoon, ladles out what he estimates to be about half the amount into the second bag. This he then ties tightly at the neck and adds to his shoebox. Then he pops all the Aspirin capsules just bought from the chemist's out onto one of two house bricks brought out from the cupboard. He slots the top brick into the bottom and presses it down so the pills are broken, ground and crushed and then applies even more weight by putting them on the floor and stepping onto it and balancing the bricks under his feet until eventually there is only a sand-like powder. Almost indistinguishable in colour and texture, he adds that to the half a kilo of genuine coke and mixes it in with the teaspoon. Then he reties the neck of the bag, slips that bag into another bag, tying that at the neck as well and laying it back in the briefcase in the bottom of his wardrobe beside the shoebox.

Creative accounting it's called. I've just made myself an extra three grand on top of the ten I gave to Karen. The ten was mine. Andy will have the potential to make thirty on the streets. It costs me a ten K investment, I sell it on to Andy for fifteen and I slip an extra three in through the back door. Andy still makes a 100% profit and I'm eight K richer.

Rob smokes a cigarette, puts his jacket back on and goes out into the main road and calls a cab.

XIII

The cab turns into Kingsway

I was homeless when I first came here, in the Dark Ages and blinded by the light, bumming and begging. The Nash told me to fuck off – no fixed abode. Washed dishes and slept in a disused railway carriage. Lived on burgers, muffins and scraps from the plates of the idle rich – literally. Until the boss of the restaurant stumbled in on me in the staff washroom giving mesel' a blanket bath in a tiny sink bollock-naked and sacked us. So I begged. There're millions afraid to look other people in the eyes. Millions. I met John busking at Charing Cross, playing his heart out for little reward. Two plus two makes dough. I took off me cap and started hassling the tourists and shoppers to cough up. And they did. It was funny how people didn't mind giving their money - as long as they could retain their conscience. We were a team. John had broken a squat in Hackney and I ended up living there. It wasn't much but it was a roof. We discovered cunning and caution. We learnt how to con, sting and hoodwink. Then I met Ally and moved in to her

gaff in Kentish Town. But there was no room for a
passenger. John never really forgave me for that. John's
world was populated by guitarists who 'sold-out' and he
endlessly criticized compromise. 'Art belongs to
everyone!' he declared and I wanted to say: 'Aye. That's
why your broke, living in a squat and busking!' But you
don't do you? You don't tell the truth. Nobody does in
this life. All your childhood and teenage years that's all
the adults say: 'Don't lie to me – tell me the truth!' But
when you get old, wise and brave enough to tell it, they
turn away and say: 'Stop making up stories!'

The cab bounces over the rutted road towards the foot of
the first of the four tower blocks. Square plaques of
various electric hues stab out randomly from the
windows that cling to the walls of the facade, climbing to
the nineteenth floor. Rob alights near a skip overflowing
with bin bags and garbage, parked alongside a burnt-out
BMW.

'You sure, mate?' grimaces the driver.

The lift door creaks open. A white man is slumped in one corner unconscious, a dark shade around his crotch and his bottom jaw hanging open. Rob steps in and presses button 13. The door closes. A few inches in front of his nose: 'Black bastards fuck off', 'NF Rule', 'Suck my dick slag'.

At the thirteenth he steps out and sends the lift with its sleeping occupant back down to the ground floor. John answers the door, sliding a number of bolts to do so. He steps in and slaps John's palm. John starts laughing.

'Jesus, you're lookin' fuckin' smart! Plenty're rich bastards down Camden eh?'

He follows John past the two rooms on the right. The first, he remembers, is John's. The second used to be his. As he passes it, he glances in and sees two men he doesn't know scrabbling in the gloom on the floor for something – just as he had done many times. One holds a lighter to see by.

'Pierre and Jacques - French bastards' says John, moving into the living room and climbing onto the beat-up plastic sofa, still there along with the black and white telly. It hasn't changed in eighteen months. Rob goes out onto the balcony and looks down at the view of Poor London. A green light flashes off and on in the sky as a jet queues up to land at Heathrow miles away to the west. John appears beside him and, undoing his flies, pisses off the edge of the balcony into the deep dark.

'Toilet fucked again?'

'Fuckin' council!' John spits.

'Where's your guitar?' Rob asks.

'Pawned it for a few days,'

'How the buskin' going? Got a recording contract yet?'

'Fuck that! Been nicked twice this month. Fuckin' bastards. Got me gear?'

'Got me dosh?'

'Don't you trust me?'

He puts the briefcase down and brings out a pink wrap from the stash in his jacket pocket. John hands him some grubby notes then looks over his shoulders and whispers: 'Don't tell them two!' then, louder: 'Make a joint!' throwing a small bag at him. Rob sees some papers and begins to build. John takes the wrap into the kitchen.

I'll stay and smoke with him. He's generally amenable after a smoke. I was all set to head down to Soho when he'd belled me and I'd thought: 'Yeah. Why not?' Nostalgia's a safe trip.

'It's always nice to see you.' says John, standing at the doorway looking in, 'Always. I was thinking about you the other day. Remember that time the old bill come to evict us? We had power then. People power. That's what counts.'

I remember telling John to let it go and him pissed and stoned raving on about 'people power', nailing flimsy planks of rotten wood across the front door and the police coming along and brushing them aside. I remember furniture raining down from the balconies on shitting-it coppers and council dudes running for their lives down below.

'Remember when we had them extermination sessions with the fucking cockroaches?'

How well I remember and how much I'd like to forget.

A microwave bell rings in the kitchen. John disappears.

It could have been me. Why did I get lucky? Is this life I've got lucky? It had to be better than how we lived. So I started working in a big hotel in The Strand, sixteen foot under the pavement, in a big kitchen, washing pots and pans, while John roamed above dreaming about record contracts and slagging musos who sold-out. I started temping for this poxy agency, done a job in the

Sally Bash gaff at Camden. Then I saw the ad in the Standard advertising for space jockeys.

'And here's one I prepared earlier!' says John, appearing in the door way again with a tiny glass pipe in one hand and a lighter in the other.

'Fuck's sake, John! Not fucking crack?'

'Paid you haven't I?'

John lights it and sucks hard on the pipe, looking as if his lungs'll explode as he fights to keep it down as long as possible.

The mobile rings. The smoke pours from John's lungs as Rob answers: it's Ben - can Rob come over at short notice? John offers the pipe. Shaking his head, he says to Ben:

'Gimme a half hour, I'll be there.'

John's hands suddenly encircle Rob's neck like talons and he lashes out and the two of them sprawl across the floor, the pipe and its burnt contents scattered. He gets to his feet and looks down at John looking up like a wounded dog, snarling, eyes popping, veins pulsing blue in his neck, saliva strung from a bottom lip pulled harsh across yellow teeth.

'You always did think you was better than me! I'm an artist! I'm no fucking angel but I believe in something. What you got? Pierre, Jacques, *ici, ici!*'

Rob tenses, not understanding what John is saying. As he looks away John kicks out and catches his calf, bringing him down on one knee. Pierre and Jacques appear, confused, looking down at them both.

'He's a dealer, boys. He's got some Charlie!'

One of them says: 'Quoi?'

'He's got cocaine! He'll give us it for free!'

The Frenchmen don't understand. They see John's pipe and sniff the air. Then they move towards him saying: 'John, you have cocaine. Give us!'

'Fuck off!' John snarls, 'It's him! He's got the coke!'

'Give us! Give us!'

'Fuck off!'

One of them grabs at John's wrists. John struggles and shouts obscenities. Rob moves quickly across the floor and up to the front door. Praying John hasn't re-bolted it, he turns the Yale and it swings open. As he runs to the stairwell and begins the descent, he hears John's voice shout: 'He's getting away, you dumb French bastards! It's him, not me!'

Leaping down each flight, three or four steps at a time, grabbing the banister, spinning around, using the impetus to leap down the next and so on, until he finally runs out at the bottom and his heart pounds as he slows from a run to a trot to a walk, across the forecourt and onto the road.

A voice calls his name in the night from a distant place, a long scream whose consonants carry on the wind and scatter like scalpels as they fall. He looks up and sees John wave from the thirteenth floor balcony.

At least, it looks like a wave.

There's a sparkle, a wink and a then bottle explodes like a hand grenade close by sending tiny shards into the night as somewhere in the dark a dog begins to bark.

Fucking madman he was!

Rob walks slowly back onto the main road, a stitch now stabbing his side. He regrets not trusting his earlier reservations about John and about not letting the inevitable wind of change brush the words under the carpet of what is gone and can never return.

XIV

When Ben opens the door to the apartment he is naked save for a pair of red silk boxer shorts and he looks half-asleep. From inside: voices, laughter and music. Ben produces some money.

'Not out here!' says Rob.

Ben opens the door wider and invites him into the short hallway. The door to the lounge is half-open - naked legs and more voices.

'You out already?' Rob asks.

'Unexpected guests, my friend, unexpected guests.'

'What you after?'

'Do me five at sixty each'

He gives Ben five pink wraps and takes six fifties.

How money should smell. Ben's been to the cash point especially. He's not talkative - he's hiding something.

The door behind Ben opens inwards and Kate appears. She has on only a t-shirt and looks as if she's been crying; her make-up and mascara have run and streaked her face.

'What's going on?' Rob asks.

Ben turns cold.

'It's none of your fucking business, mate.'

'We've known each two years and you talk to me like that?'

Kate presses herself against him and whispers in his ear:

'Have you ever been in love?'

He thinks about it for only a split second and then replies quietly: 'Yes'

'What's it like? I've forgotten'

Her fingernails dig into his palm.

Then the lounge door opens wide and standing in the doorway is another woman Rob has never seen before but she's topless, huge pendulous tits hanging on her chest and in her hands she holds a video camera, filming everything.

'What's going on?' big tits asks.

'Do you want to fuck her?' Ben asks, nodding at Kate.

'The tape's running,' says big tits.

In seconds Rob is on the street and looking for a cab.

XV

Rob opens his eyes and blinks down at the empty bottle lying on its side at his feet. There is a faded telephone number scrawled on his hand. His watch says a quarter to seven. Daylight is filtering through the frosted glass of the room he is in. His head moves – he's lying in a bath. The frosted glass is the glass of a shower door. It is not his bathroom. He does not recognise it and of course he doesn't even have to move his eyes to see. He knows. He is naked. A voice shouts his name. He stands up slowly - but still slips on the enamel sides, jarring elbows and knees, slithering and sliding. Oxygen seeps into the space behind his eyes but not fast enough. A sprinkling of tiny stars cloud the blackness of his vision.

He steps clumsily out and slips again, crashing down in no uncertain order onto the floor of the bathroom. He lifts the lid of a wicker laundry basket and plunges his arms deep into the soiled washing, pulling out an armful of dirty socks, knickers, bras, underpants, t-shirts and jeans. Clutching them to his chest, he falls against the bathroom door, slides the little gold bolt.

Nigel and two girls stare at him.

'I'm going to make myself a bed,' he mumbles.

Nigel shakes his head and laughs and then takes the washing, stepping past him and dropping the pile back into the laundry basket. The girls smile and turn away.

'Put some fucking clothes on – preferably your own!' advises Nigel.

'Where are they?' Rob asks.

'Stay there!'

He stays where he is and Nigel disappears. Rob puts in a formal request to his brain: to search its memory banks for what events brought him to where he is now.

Jesus, I feel like I've jumped off a high diving board and still haven't reached the water.

Nigel re-appears, holding his clothes, a spliff dangling from his lower lip. Rob takes the spliff and sucks on it. His tight lungs reject the smoke and he doubles over coughing. Resting his hands on the edge of the basin, he suddenly pukes - a mouthful of what looks like orange and yellow cardboard into the sink. Nigel grimaces.

'What happened?'

'Get dressed an' I'll fill you in. Meantime, I really am desperate to use the kharzi, mate!'

Rob is pushed out onto the landing and dresses slowly and clumsily like a child, clothes damp with sweat and the stink of booze and smoke. He pats his jeans and is relieved to feel his house keys still there. By the time he's completely dressed, Nigel has finished, flushing the toilet and re-opening the bathroom door.

'Jesus' sighs Nigel 'Are you on a fuckin' suicide mission or something?'

He is pushed down the stairs to the basement kitchen where he takes a seat at a pine kitchen table and bench, piled with empty beer cans, a cheese plant and a full ashtray. One of the girls appears in the kitchen doorway. She is blond. Then the other appears behind her, another blonde. Both cautiously enter the kitchen and stand close to Nigel as he makes coffee, eyeing Rob like two sparrows at one hawk. Fear, evident by its lack of great detail, enters through one ear and out of the other, the space between: a vacuum.

'So, last night you was at Kerry's do in Shoreditch, remember?' asks Nigel.

'Was I?'

'You got fucked up and then we all ended up back here. We done a load of powder and then you rush in Nina's room, rip your kit off and start screaming: 'A'right, gels, who's first?' Remember?'

'Where's me jacket?' Rob asks.

'No jacket,' says Nigel.

'You're fucking joking?'

'Nina? Cindy? You remember any jacket?'

Nina shakes her head. Cindy shrugs. Nigel turns away. Nobody cares.

'Where's me boots?'

'Under the table' says Nigel pointing.

Rob finds them and goes straight to the two secret compartments - both bring out a total of about a grand.

Well it's not all bad news. I've lost me jacket. I've lost me mobile and I've lost me stash but according to how much money I've still got in me boots I must have sold most of me gear before losing what was left.

'I've lost me mobile and me jacket.'

'Too bad, mate,' says Nigel, not really caring.

'What day is it?'

'Sunday' says Nigel, handing over a mug of coffee.

'What happened last night? What did I do?'

Nigel and me had met and dropped some E's. Business had been brisk. Karen had turned up later on with Billy. A DJ called Wendy had taken them into a back room and snorted lines of snow and knocked back Tequilas and Scotch for a bit before doing another E. Then somebody had tipped up with some acid. Nigel had declined, recognising his limits but Rob had dropped one. He'd returned with Nigel, Nina and Cindy 'cause Nina, in her E state, confessed she was horny enough to shag both Nigel and him and Cindy at the same time. So I'd stripped off and jumped on the bed and started bouncing up and down shouting: 'Who's first?' Unfortunately by that time the E's were wearing off, so they'd all started to come down to reality. I then drunk mesel' into a stupor and fall asleep in the bathroom, much to everyone's annoyance 'cause I'd also locked the door so nobody could use the toilet and three of them had to piss in the back garden.

Nina steps forward and holds something out to him. It's a Polaroid. It shows a photo of what looks like an orangutan, a half bottle in one hand, the other wrapped around its dick, a gormless grin on its face, frozen in space.

'Thanks for the memory' says Cindy sarcastically.

'You're sure I didn't bring me jacket back?'

'Have a look!' says Nigel.

Rob searches the house - nothing. He makes a decision. He opens the front door and finds himself in a deserted street of new semis with a building site for a garden. The sun is shining.

'Where the fuck am I?'

'Bromley-by-Bow'

'What the fuck does that mean?'

'That means: go west for five or six miles then north for five or six and you'll be closer to Camden.'

'I've lost me jacket and me mobile, Nige. I'm in seriously bad shit.'

'For a dealer, yes you are.'

'What am I gonna do?'

'Get another one?'

Rob walks along the pavement, not looking back. An empty road, a few parked cars. Over to his left, at some distance, a car door slams shut. Above the new estate, distant but dominating, a red light winks from the summit of Canary Wharf against the backdrop of an early morning sunrise. He cannot explain why or whether he's justified in doing so but he walks faster, seeking signs of life. The order, from the brain to the legs, is slow to impact. He looks behind and sees a man standing next to a car. Spotting a 'phone booth, he goes into it but swears when he sees the receiver has been ripped out. He walks on. Another junction. To the left a closed garage, a railway bridge, to the right a small park where an early morning man walks his dog. He walks a little faster. The dog walker looks and the dog lifts its head and barks once. He walks across the road onto a paved precinct. Canary Tower's plate windows reflect the rising sun's reflection on surrounding city buildings. Figures move around not too far away. Rob stops and looks back only for a second and sees a car, the same car, moving – is it moving? He goes into a newspaper shop, and, once inside, sneaks a peek outside through the window as the car - a grey-blue Volvo cruises past. His instinct is to reach for his mobile and call Camden Cab Company but he has no mobile. That with which he is so familiar is absent.

He casts a glance in the direction the Volvo took but sees nothing so he leaves the shop and walks on, by now the shadow of the Tower cast across him.

The road joins another, funnelling narrowly to where a few vehicles turn a roundabout. A black cab lurches into view and he waves, making the cab brake hard and the car behind do the same.

'Camden Town!'

Glancing at him once as his fare slips down in the seat and angles to scout from the rear window, the cabby moves forward as other vehicles weave into and out of its path, camouflaging it in a convoy of colour.

XVI

A waitress brings the mug on a tray and puts it down in front of him without a word, without a glance. Conveniently sitting near the door, Rob's eyes scout the street. A policeman stands across the way in shirtsleeves.

On the long journey back Rob asked the cabbie to stop at the end of his road rather than outside his building. This had been a wise move - a Volvo was parked outside his door, with an occupant.

'Where to?' the driver inquires.

Camden Parkway was the destination chosen. He found a cafe he liked and was now pondering his next move: how to get back into his flat. Who the driver of the Volvo was didn't matter. What a man doesn't know can't hurt him. Rob attracts the waitress' attention.

'Do you have a 'phone?'

She points towards the toilets. Rob goes out and sees the box fixed to the wall. He lifts the receiver.

Karen's number is oh, two – shit. Cannot remember it. Everything's on the mobile and the mobile's lost.

He hangs up. His head is starting to pound. A hangover, which has delayed itself whilst he deals with reality, is catching up. His brain is overloaded with chemicals, unable to accurately tell him whether he is hot or cold, hungry or full, tired or alert, confused or clear. He returns to his table and looks into his coffee.

Brain needs vitamins, calcium, protein, iron not nicotine, alcohol or heroin. So what's the plan? Is there a plan? I live like a Spartan after all. I've done moonlight flits before. Remember Maida Vale? I'm an expert at the moonlight flit.

Rob goes to the counter and buys a packet of cigarettes and the waitress hands him a free book of matches with his change on a saucer. Taking them, he returns to his table. A young couple have seated themselves opposite.

Speaking in some foreign tongue, they smile at him and speak but he doesn't understand and smiles back. They unfold a map of London on the table and point at landmarks.

If I could get in to the flat, pack me stuff and get out again I could shack up in a hotel for a few days, weeks, then get mesel' a new pad someplace. I have to get in! I've got Andy to sort! I've got to get him that half key.

Dropping some coins on the table, Rob stands and goes out into the street. The pavements flow with optimistic pedestrians but a bruised and sullen sky rolls overhead, warning of the folly of expecting good weather and quickly blotting out the sun.

Names and faces flow through Rob's memory. He turns each one around, seeking a face that might be able to help him with the most immediate problem: how to get back into his apartment.

XVII

'Did you fuck 'er?'

'No' says Rob, putting his hand on his chest in the place he thought his heart was.

Not because I didn't want to but because I fucking couldn't.

Jeremy looks at him for a second, rubs his eyes, yawns and goes into the kitchen where he fills a kettle.

'I don't give a fuck anyway. So what's this all about? It's not often you need summat from me?'

'I'm in a jam. I need to get into me flat, get something and then get out again without the person who's waiting for me in their car outside knowing I've been there.'

'What person?'

'I don't know and I don't care. The less I know the longer I live.'

Jeremy yawns and pulls his robe tighter around himself.

'Have you got any powder?'

'I've lost me stash.'

'Fucking hell, things are going well for you today aren't they?'

'So, what can I do?'

'Is it Plod?'

Rob shrugs.

'I'm a respected Guardian journalist. I mean, I always thought our relationship was business, not personal. If it is Plod then it's personal.'

'I'm not asking you to marry me. I'm just looking for some ideas.'

'On your own, mate!'

Rob smashes his right fist into the left side of Jeremy's head. Jeremy reels back, putting up his hand. Rob looks down at his knuckles - the skin has scraped white with the impact, exposing a depth of pink flesh turning rapidly crimson.

'Fuck!'

A woman's voice from another part of his apartment calls Jeremy's name. Without looking back, Rob walks straight out of the door and into the street. He looks down at his knuckles. Round wet drops of rain fall on him from a yellow sky as he goes down the main road in the direction of Primrose Hill, shaking the pain out of his fist and passing a newsagent's billboard that reads: ECSTASY GIRL IN COMA.

Amoc ni lrig ysatsce. Whichever way I say it – no effect. I sell hundreds, thousands of pills. So what? Did I force anyone to buy them, force them to take them? So a drunken driver kills a kid. Is it the barman's fault for serving the driver the booze? Who the fuck thinks they're gonna live forever? Show me them. Where are they, the Immortals? Drugs are about as likely to kill you as any other fucking thing in this world.

He sees a 'phone booth.

I want to dial George's number but can't remember it. Fuck, fuck, fuck!

The rain stops, the sun shines, a rainbow forms. Dogs frolic in the grass as mothers and fathers share pushchairs and kids toddle along then stop to pick up daisies.

Falling in love is easy. Falling out of it is scary. It's like putting all your money on the same horse and the fucker loses. It's a terrifying ride after: drugs, booze, pubs and bars. Everything that could be taken, I took. Everything that could be drunk, I drank. Was it to forget? Or was forgetting just an excuse to get fucked up? I have no answers.

Rob collapses heavily on a bench halfway up the hill. At the bottom is Regent's Park Zoo and then Central London, Oxford Street, Westminster, those places. He pinpoints the dome of St. Paul's.

We walked to the top many moons ago. It was dead romantic - she waited 'till we were alone and then got down on her knees and sucked me off.

Two figures wander in front of him and pause, blocking his view. The woman turns, sees Rob and comes to him, holding out a camera.

'You take picture us, please?'

It's the couple from the cafe in Parkway. Get out of my face. I'm too busy feeling lost, alien, like I don't really live here at all, like it's all some mad fucking day trip. London does that to me. Be warned: weeks, days melt behind, tumbling dominoes. Dealing reduces memory to one or two days in either direction of the here and now. Reality is reality. You can't conduct straight-minded principles when you're wrecked out of your box. Without a memory it's easy to lie. Invent dreams and feelings to suit the mood.

A flash of metal catches his eye and he halts as Fuzzy skids alongside, still on his stolen mountain bike. He opens the carrier bag he's carrying and motions Rob to look inside.

'Top of the range CD's: still wrapped, freshly nicked. U2, Trance, Hendrix, Sixties, a fiver to you, a bargain!'

'Fuzzy, how'd you like to earn some cash?'

'Fucking stupid question!'

Fuzzy chains his bike to some railings. Rob takes off Fuzzy's red baseball cap. It has a dull stain of sweat on the inside band. He pulls it onto his own head then finds a taxi and asks the driver to wait at the end of the road and keep the engine running, giving him a ten to keep him sweet. Rob gives Fuzzy a ten and tells him to jump in the cab on Rob's signal and to keep the driver of the Volvo going for as long as the ten lasts.

'And the rest!' says Fuzzy. Rob gives him another ten.

'And me dying grandma!' says Fuzzy. Rob hands him another ten.

Rob and Fuzzy turn the corner of Rob's street. Rob strides towards the blue Volvo. The driver, head down, reads a newspaper. As Rob gets nearer, the driver looks up. Rob stops. The driver half opens the door of the car. Rob turns and trots back from the direction he's come. The driver gets back into his car and reaches forward to the ignition. Rob returns the baseball cap to Fuzzy and tells him to jump into the cab as Rob ducks down behind a small pile of bin bags. The Volvo appears and Rob sees the Oriental driver search the faces of the crowd, resting his gaze on a red baseball cap in the back of a cab - sticking two fingers up. The Volvo lurches into the traffic in as hot a pursuit as slow moving traffic can allow.

Rob, heart suddenly pounding, runs into his road, over the grass and up to his front door. Fumbling with his keys, the door falls inwards, slams it hard behind him and collapses to the carpet.

Hong Kong Phooey can fuck right off.

XVIII

Fucking refugee. No time to waste. Change of clothes. Suitcase out. Pull out the drawers and tip them straight in, jackets, shirt, shoebox, briefcase, shaving foam, razors, toothbrush, tapes, CD's, loose money – all goes in the suitcase. Unplug the CD player and 'phone the cab office. Fuck it! I do not have a mobile! I need a line. No, not a 'phone line! A white line will help to keep my head cool. Here we go, here we go, here we go. Come to Daddy. Oh yes! Hmm. Feels so good. Thirty years of life in a suitcase. Thirty years up me nose. Get out of here before Hong Kong Fooey comes back. Ahmed. Take me up West, a nice five star hotel some place with maids, butlers, room service. I'll tell them I'm in the music business, that always impresses people when they ask me what I do for a living, of course I never say 'I'm a drug dealer', that'd be very, very silly. Shower, relax, shave, pull on some cool togs and take a nice leisurely down to Andy's in Balham, do this deal, get fucked and hey – tomorrow's another day. Tomorrow I'm gonna be somebody else. Who am I gonna be tomorrow? Well whoever I am I'd better get myself some SOTA telecoms and get connected. Fancy a laptop to plug in to surf the porno channels. Okay son. You're ready. Keys? Yes, keys. Pop them in an envelope and a little note: 'Dear Mister Estate Agent . . . ' God, you are such a fucking vet, my friend, though do yourself a favour and just check through that spy hole first before opening the door.

His life in a suitcase on the carpet beside him, Rob suddenly finds himself looking at an Oriental man with shoulder-length black hair and a grey summer suit.

Why am I not surprised?

XIX

I'm scared of the black umbrella that spreads over England ragged as a raven pecking for carrion for I'll be nothing but a scrap to be torn by its beak. Violence and pain are on the margins with me everyday, amplified here.

The Oriental has his back to the front door. He turns and puts his face close to the spy hole. The doorbell rings persistently. The visitor then takes a mobile out and dials a number. As he begins to speak, he walks away from the door, looking up at the house. Rob puts his suitcase down and goes back into his living room. It still looks as if there's been a party that hasn't been cleaned up. He glances out across his back lawn.

And when I close me eyes and open them again everything will be just how it was yesterday: perfect, no clouds on the horizon, spotless, simple. I'll turn into a ghost and float out the front door and past me unwanted and unwelcome visitor.

He lets himself out onto the patio and stands on the dustbin and looks over the wall into Simon's lounge. Simon's patio door is open. He climbs over and taps on the window. Simon looks out of the shadows, surprised.

'Simon, can I use your 'phone?'

XX

Cutting a gap in the curtain, Rob finds himself confronted by Alana who in turn holds a carrier bag stuffed with soft materials. Behind him hovers a curious Simon. Rob flicks the lever that opens the patio doors.

As Alana steps in, she asks: 'Are things really that bad?'

'Like I said on the 'phone' says Rob.

'First, I need the loo,'

Alana goes off to the toilet. Simon leans forward.

'Blimey, that your bird?'

'Thanks for letting me use the 'phone, Si.'

'No problem, Rob. Glad to be of help!'

'Surfer Simon' I call him. Doesn't smoke, drink, do drugs. For kicks Simon does sport. I've no idea where his income comes from.

'So what's going on exactly?'

'You know Si I've an expression that I live by.'

'Yeah?'

'It goes something like: what you don't know you can't be beaten out of you.'

Simon holds up his hands in a gesture of surrender.

'As you like. Look, I'm gonna go back to my pad. Gimme a shout when you need me, okay?'

As Simon climbs back over the dividing wall, the toilet flushes and Alana comes out, straightening her tight dress. She raises an eyebrow and casts a glance around.

'So this is where it all happens?'

The arc of a pendulum is the limit of my sanity. I am entertaining a coke-snorting tranny.

Alana tiptoes up to the front door and looks through the spy hole.

'I don't think anyone saw me go into Simon's. There's certainly no one there now.'

'You said you on the 'phone had a plan?'

Alana pushes the carrier bag into Rob's arms.

'Put these on!'

Rob opens the bag and looks inside. Then he looks back at Alana.

'This is your plan?'

'Do you have a better one?'

'No way!'

'I should be working now. You're costing me money.'

Rob goes into the bathroom and locks the door then tips the contents of the bag onto the floor.

So that's why he asked me my shoe size.

XXI

As Rob takes a deep breath and steps out of the bathroom, he expects Alana to collapse in hysterics but instead Alana studies what she sees seriously, snaps her fingers and says: 'Make-up!'

She takes some mascara from her handbag and approaches Rob, tipping his head back.

'Look at me. Don't make faces. Question.'

'Go on'

'Tits?'

'I like tits.'

'That wasn't my question'

'About two and half grand in each cup.'

Alana applies the eyeliner to Rob's eyelashes then produces lipstick and makes him purse his lips so she can paint them bright red. Rob looks in the bathroom mirror. Tumbling about his shoulders and face is a blond wig that frames his eyes and mouth. On his feet are black platform shoes a size too small but enough to hobble a few yards. His trousers are baggy and made of black cotton and over them hangs a red shirt fastened up to the collar. Alana takes two earrings from her handbag and clips them onto his ears.

'While you were getting changed I spoke with Simon. I think he's taken a shine to me. Congratulations, Robert, you've got your uses. I do like his Porsche. Let me have a look at you. Hmm: two tall women, one with huge shoulders. Try a walk.'

Without trying at all, Rob walks across the room and back again. The shoes force him to pay extra attention to his step and gait.

'No, no, no, lead from the hip and try and imagine there's a room full of beautiful women all dying for you to shag them. So make sure they could a good eyeful of your ass and your cock.'

Crumbling with embarrassment, Rob does so. Alana hands Rob the spare handbag she's brought and hooks it over his shoulder.

'Okay - we'll walk out by Simon's front door. The car doors will be open. You pull your suitcase along on the wheels.'

'What about my CD player?'

'Fuck it. Get in on the passenger side. It's only a few metres from the front door to the car. Stay upright, take small steps and lead from the hip. Put these on!'

Alana produces a pair of sunglasses. Rob puts them on and Alana exits via the patio. She slips off her shoes and clambers like the man she truly is over the wall.

Rob casts one last glance around the place that's been his home for the last few months. He wonders if he should feel something but he doesn't and can't. He rearranges the curtain to make it look as if it was arranged from inside and pulls the patio door closed, confident that his hunters will inevitably end up inside the apartment sooner or later. He slips off the platform shoes and pulls himself up onto the wall, lowering himself down the other side and stepping into Simon's lounge. Simon is about to speak but Rob waves a finger and says: 'Don't!'

Simon, Alana and Rob go to the front door. Alana opens it a little and looks out.

'Simon: go out to your car, open the drivers door and then open the boot. Come back here, take Rob's case, put it in the boot and close it. Then come back in the house. Don't look around, don't look anywhere. Just do it. All right lovely?'

Simon does as he's asked and returns.

'I'm going first. Simon: you come out first and walk ahead of me, I'll be right behind you. Rob, you'll be right behind me. Simon will open the passenger door then push the seat forward and I'll get in the back. Rob will get in the front and Simon'll close the door. Then Simon'll get behind the wheel, start the engine and reverse out. If there's any talking to be done, let me do it. Got it? Good luck!' Alana then touches Rob's arm and squeezes gently.

'Remember: back straight, small steps, lead from the hips. And if that doesn't work – I'll smack the fucker in the mouth, okay?'

Alana opens the door. Simon walks out to the car, following the instructions. Rob steps out into the light and tries to remember his own instructions. His heart is pounding. The wig is making his scalp itch. The straps of the bra are chaffing his shoulders and back and the false tits, though not heavy, are very disconcerting.

I'm gonna get a job! Go straight! Support the police! Learn a proper trade! Help old people across the road! Give to charity! Pay me taxes! Vote! Pray! I promise, I promise, I promise! Just get me out of this!

Ahead of him Simon holds open the passenger door and looks towards them anxiously. Simon is aware Rob hasn't followed Alana's instructions, but understands – he too would have a problem walking out into the world dressed like that! Simon also knows it'll attract attention if Alana gets out again and tries to persuade Rob to be brave, so Simon speaks to Alana and then comes back to the front door.

'She says: Leave with us or stay here. It's your choice.'

'Look at me, for Christ's sake! Look at me!' Rob says bitterly.

'Be brave, Rob, just be brave!'

Rob takes another deep breath, sticks out his chest and steps out into the daylight.

'Man-dressed-as-woman' written all over me. I've felt vulnerable before in me life but nothing like this - great for the scrapbook.

Although it seems like eternity, it's only a few paces and a few seconds to the car. Rob skirts the open door and whispers: 'Thanks, pet' to Simon and is about to climb in with all the grace of a gorilla when he hears Alana hiss:

'Not like a fucking squaddie!'

Rob lowers himself into the seat, the tits making him manoeuvre cautiously. Simon whispers: 'Fingers!' and slams the door, skipping around, getting behind the wheel, closing his door and starting the engine.

'Pretend to be laughing!' Alana whispers from the back seat.

Rob smiles blandly. The car reverses and pulls forward, passing the stationary blue Volvo, behind the wheel the Oriental who spares them only a cursory glance, is preoccupied with his mobile.

At the end of the road Simon asks: 'Which way?'

Alana leans forward in the back seat so that Rob can feel her breath on his ears and whispers: 'Which way would you like to go, darling?'

'The *fuck* out of here!' says Rob.

XXII

In the small medicine cupboard above the sink is evidence of Alana's *alter ego*: a Phillip's Ladyshave and an unopened box of tampons. Rob shaves.

I really got in to be driven around London in a Porsche looking like a rich slag. It's great being somebody else. I hated reality when I was younger. Reality made me into me, Rob Barlow. Nobody. Nobody, nowhere. So I took drugs to change my reality. Now the reality I thought I could escape into has become my new reality. It's no longer a part-time leisure activity - it's a fulltime occupation. Maybe it's time I started being that kid again? What was his name again? Robert Barlow? What happened to him? He was sixteen, seventeen. He had a career; it wasn't much, a graphic designer in a tiny office North East of Nowhere. Middlesbrough. Middlesbrough. Not much but something. He went out with the lads Friday and Saturday nights down Albert Road. If they were flush they drove over to Darlo or spent the early hours at Tall Trees near Yarm. Getting out of it was an occasional thing not a fulltime job.

Robert Barlow's idea of pleasure used to be sticking a tent in a backpack over his shoulders and trekking off to the Dales for a few nights with a freshly cashed giro in his wallet. He lit campfires and wrote poetry in the sunset. Whatever happened to Robert Barlow?

I could go to Andalusia and lie on a beach for a few weeks. Why not? Done it before a few years back. Why not? 'coz I'd attract the wrong sort of people. I just would. I'd be introduced to the local mafia and soon I'd be ferrying boats of hashish across the Straits of Gibraltar from Morocco or shipping in cocaine from Puerto Rico. No. Money's not the glue that's holding these mad events together. It's finding something useful to do with me life, some reason to wake up in the morning, that's the key.

In time all will be revealed. But life is fucking rubbish let's face it. I want to feel as beautiful as E and snow makes me feel all the time. I don't want to get old and tired and a has-been or a once-was. I'll not end up in a bed-sit, signing on, claiming Housing Benefit, darning me socks, wanking off when pretty young schoolgirls walk past me window and pissing in the sink because I cannat be arsed to walk up to the communal bog. I see it often: I'm on me deathbed. God sits on the end eyeing me up, looking at his watch, drumming his fingers impatiently. I say: 'You'll be waiting a long fucking time, pal!' I can't win. It's all rigged. Gear wakes up a tedious life. Drugs and cash and sex and dancing are better than love and making a living and getting old. Reality is fucking shite. Love is fucking shite. You fall in love with a firm pair of tits, a cute backside, a tight pussy, that's love.

Replacing the shaver, Rob stuffs the money into his cowboy boots, picks up the clothes he wore in the car and unlocks the bathroom door. Simon and Alana are giggling and turn silent when they see Rob. Rob holds out Alana's clothes and asks: 'What shall I do with these?'

Alana takes them through to his bedroom. Simon whispers: 'Alana's a really nice lady, Rob!'

Rob sees his suitcase on the floor and goes to it, opening it as he talks to Simon.

'Lady?' Rob asks.

'Yeah, lady. She's not some common-or-garden slapper. She's got attitude, man!'

Does Alana get a gold star for presentation or what does Simon know? I mean does he know? Maybe he does know and doesn't care? That makes him cooler than I thought.

'Thanks for your help. I appreciate it.'

'Does this mean you and me ain't gonna be neighbours no more?'

'Kind of,'

'Shame. Will I see you again?'

'I'll pop in for tea and biscuits wearing a false beard and glasses,'

'What'll I tell the landlord?'

'Tell him - and anyone else who asks I had to go abroad - urgently.'

Simon holds out his hand to shake.

'Don't be a stranger, Rob.'

We're all strangers, Simon.

Rob finds his briefcase and zips up the suitcase again. Alana appears.

'Off so soon?'

'I've got business, down to Balham and after that over to Wandsworth. Is it okay to leave this till I get sorted?'

'Where will you stay tonight?'

'I'll find a hotel. I'll bell you.'

'You don't have a mobile,'

'I'll buy one and you'll be the first to have me number,'

Rob throws his denim jacket over his arm, picks up the briefcase and lets himself out.

XXIII

Rob lies on the grass in the shade of some trees while all around is the perpetual humming of the city machine. Clouds within clouds, barely moving, wait for something to happen. The sun, past its apex, begins its slow descent from the sky, pulling down with it fingers of red and frying the earth, making it sticky and stale.

Except it's not moving is it? The sun I mean. It's still. It's us moving. It's a delusion, an illusion. I'm an educated man. I'm not an uneducated man. How am I going to get started again? Am I going to get started again? Karen. What will she do? Where will she go? All those numbers filed into the memory of me lost mobile. I could let them blow away like dust. That mobile represents the past. No. Somewhere in me suitcase they're jotted down in a notebook, most of them anyway. Where am I going to stay tonight? I am a passenger, I ride and I ride. No, even Iggy's got an accountant. Respect. Purity. Dignity. I'm naming each cloud as it drifts along. I'm reaching out. I want to court dizziness as I stand at the abyss, teetering on the edge, that frightening time and space between safety and common sense, between certain death and certain immortality, a no-grace performance for the cheap seats. The toilet cubicle doors open and lock behind me automatically as I fall in. 'Stay there, wastrel!' 'Know your place!' 'Know your station!' The voices will say. 'And do what?' I'll throw back at them. Qualifications? None. Never stopped me from getting what I deserved. Actions are the real tools, not words. School was all so pre-planned, organised, ready, waiting. The system is fucking ruthless - judge, jury, executioner. Growing up is like getting bits forcibly ripped out but hey, humankind has learnt to live with its shortcomings. Put on a brave face. I learned nowt, zero, zilch - except one thing: everything new is instantly old as soon as it's understood. Reality is compromise, struggle, suffering, heartache, trapped loyalties, divided opinions, bad backs, false teeth and hair loss.

Outside the block in Balham, a porter in shirtsleeves steps forward to open the cab door. Rob gets out and looks up; its entrance flanked with marble pillars,

Victoriana and sculpted Union Jack-waving lions sporting crowns.

Paying the cabbie, the porter waves him through into the Reception, marble floors and thick green plants tall and slender in the coffee-coloured light of an evening that glows through high windows. A large fan turns lazily overhead, cooling him for a second as he goes towards the lift. Finding Andy's name on the brass panel, he presses the button alongside.

'Yeah?'

'Andy?'

'Great timing. Come up, you know where it is.'

Andy and me met while working for a publishing company, selling advertising space for Ben. Ben's 'daddy' was some rich twat who'd never had to work for a living and whose ancestors made a fortune paying northern plebs a pittance to break their backs down the mines. Ben's 'daddy' had set up his son in the manner to which he was accustomed, i.e. doing as little as necessary for as much as possible. Sales were down one time so I started feeding the powder to Andy and Ben and suddenly sales soared. Money pours in. Then there's a dry patch and sales plummet. So we pool our dough and move into dealing. There's this mass exodus from Ben's but there was no hard feelings for Ben 'cause the supply of gear was more important to him. He went into voluntary liquidation and wrote all his debts through the limited status, stashing what was in the company account in an offshore bank. Andy dealt for a little while but then slipped back into advertising. He said he missed the office routine and the friendships. Only me, only I stayed the course.

Andy says: you wake up, you get high, you get old and then you die. I like that. It's stuck with me like an underground song. Fifteen hundred ten pound notes. That's some wad. I'll buy a Polaroid and take a self-portrait chucking it up in the air and watching 'em tumble down round me like that bird in 'Spend, Spend, Spend'. Who will I be next: a freelance computer technician, an executive head-hunter, a rock star or the

illegitimate son of a famous face? Get a gaff in
Kensington and have some High Court judge as a
neighbour, peddling Charlie to the cunt's daughter at
Roedean. She can pay by nicking from mummy's purse.
When you're nobody you can be anybody! All suckers'll
lick spittle for the colour of money.

When Andy opens the door he is holding up a video
camera. Rob closes his palm over the lens.

'Alright, mate, cool it, this is expensive tackle!'

'I don't wanna be on your fucking holiday snaps!'

'Point taken. You see any tarts down there?'

'No'

'Shame. I hired some slags. That's what the camera's for
- stick some Charlie down their necks and off we fucking
go, my son!'

They go through to the kitchen. A house tune thumps through from the living room. Andy pulls up two high stools at a small worktop. Rob places the briefcase on his knees, opens the lid and brings out the half K bag. He puts the briefcase down on the floor and smirks with some private satisfaction as Andy's eyes widen.

I expect a much better hit than I'm getting right now. I expect to feel powerful, important, and useful. Power is all about possession: who has it and who wants it.

'How many Aspirins you put in there?'

'Fuck off!' says Rob.

'Fair question, Rob. I'll need to know these things if I'm gonna make it last.'

'I wouldn't do such a thing,' Rob lies.

'No, of course you wouldn't.'

Andy reaches over to a pot marked TEA and brings out three thick orange rolls that he pushes over.

'Five hundred tens - three times!'

Rob glances at the money.

'You gonna count it?' Andy asks.

'What you do with this gear, Andy, is your business. If anything fucks up – and I mean anything – it never, ever comes back to me right?'

'Right!'

'No. I said: 'Right?' right?'

'Right!'

There - sounded like a fucking idiot but covered me back. I'll tell you exactly what me police statement will say:

'Andy who? Never heard of the twat.'

'How long we known each other, Rob? There's a dozen turds on my floor'll pay top dollar for this every time they get on the dog. It's an investment.'

I remember dishwashing. I remember cleaning bogs out. I remember that ad in the Standard. Why did I ever answer that fucking ad in the fucking Evening Standard? It was that fucking wino's fault - if he hadn't pissed all over the fucking floor instead of down the fucking pan, I'd never've seen that fucking ad. First week: no sales. Second week: no sales. Third week: Ben says: 'Have a toot on this number, Rob!' and wham, bam, up your ham, three hundred quid walks into me pocket! And then Ben takes me out and gets me fucked and asks: 'So, what have you come to London for, all the way from sunny Teesside?' and I joke: 'To get a serious cocaine habit!' 'coz it was half-meant as a joke, but if it was only half meant as a joke then I guess the other half was meant as serious. Oh what a wit the little tyke has, so devil-may-care and cavalier.

Andy produces a bottle of champagne and two glasses.

'I was saving this for later but fuck it!'

He pops the cork and two glasses fizz to their brims.

'To success!'

They toast and the glasses clink then Andy says: 'Better give this a spin before them birds turn up - one for the road? They might be right fucking dogs. Bit of this down us and they'll look like Claudia fucking Schiffer!'

Rob takes the elastic band off the first wad and begins to count. Andy opens the half-kilo bag at the neck and brings out a small amount that he puts onto the worktop. He arranges two clumsy lines with the edge of the spoon and then rolls up a twenty. Then he offers Rob the note. Rob pauses in his count and snorts the line. His eyes water and then the powder trampolines his head across the room, bounces it off the wall and back onto his shoulders. Andy takes the note and also snorts.

'Jesus! That is fucking good! Let's rock and fucking roll!'

Can I feel the Aspirin?

Rob looks again at the wad. The thought of recounting what he's already counted seems suddenly daunting, uninteresting, boring. The doorbell rings and Andy goes out to answer it. Rob takes the three wads and shoves them casually into his jacket pocket. Then he goes out to the hallway and turns off into the toilet, locking the door behind him. He pulls down his jeans and sits on the seat. Beyond the door he can hear female voices.

Me heart is pumping fit to burst. I feel horny, I don't feel horny, I want to shit, I don't want to shit, I want to fuck and I don't.

A squeal and a giggle come through from the kitchen. The thumping house music is notched up in volume, the bass vibrating through the toilet wall.

Time is coming, Party man. Open up. Go. Seek. Impress, saviour. Whores will lap you up because you hold the key. It's all about power. Who has and who wants. It takes a whore to know a whore. Tell them about your dull and uneventful day. That joke isn't funny anymore you wastrel, you performer of little grace for the cheap seats. This is it. This is your Shite Life. Surrender to the drug. Abandon hope all ye who enter here. Care for nobody. Be unfeeling. If you don't care, you can't hurt. Stoned, drunk, orgasm, paper, money, pain, numb, rage.

'Oy - what you doing in there, wanking? Some gels here wanna give you a hand!'

Waiting for something to happen. I'm waiting for something to happen. I'm waiting - for something - to happen. I've got fifteen fucking thousand pounds in my pocket and another bunch someplace else. I have power. I am on top of me little world and yet I feel nothing. Andy doesn't understand - I do this every fucking day. For Andy it's a novelty. He's not organised like me, I'm organised. So you wanna party, Andy? Want to walk in the clouds and fly in the sky? All right, mate, all right.

Rob wades back into the kitchen. Two girls stand in front of him. He cannot see their faces and though he hears the names instantly forgets. Andy proffers a mirror with carefully laid-out lines and the girls are smoking, glancing nervously at them. A third girl says Andy is on her way up, parking the car. Rob ignores the mirror and opening the neck of the bag pushes his face into the powder and sucks it into his lungs.

The girls. The girls are gaping at me white face. Andy is a picture! Me head fills with exploding veins. The dust falls down onto me shirt and collects in me mouth like sherbet. I grab the champagne and suck. Bubbles burst out through me nose, splattering gobbets of coke and snot on anything within five feet. Powder and booze squeeze vertical. Drowning, I'm drowning in cocaine and champagne. What a fucking epitaph. I am one with God. I am all the Gods. Games. Bullshit. Wasting time. The point! The point! What is the fucking point? Bitch. Whore. Slag. Roar. I groan. I am a wounded man, a wounded animal. Starting to kick in that bass, my cock, God's cock - in front of every – ceased to - teetered in

that limbo place - me and the tart - want to be inside her,
where is -

Rob pulls a girl by the wrist down the hallway into the first bedroom, slamming the door behind him. She backs away into a corner.

'Stop, stop!' she's whispering. 'I don't know!'

'Sure you know, baby!'

Pull at her shirt. There is resistance. It's natural. She wants to, doesn't want to, likes control and hates it. The Coke Monster roars. Listen to it. Let it's voice tear away your defences. Surrender to it, pet. Wants it - doesn't – enjoys it – shouldn't – pull at her shirt - lips, nipples, fingers, the smell of pussy, the taste of piss – rip off her pants, tight that - to her knees - fall on top of - legs open - enough to - kick me off. Now she's trapped. Why resist? Let the demon take control. What's your name again? Feel that? Block everything out.

'What about AIDS? What about protection?'

I'll protect you! I'm the saviour. I can heal the sick and give life to the dead. Don't move it's time for entry. Let me in, I wanna go home! In space no one can hear you prevaricate. Strong aren't I?

'No!'

Fuck, you're dry girl. Up we go, invader. Snarl at me? Snarl at me? Spit, spit! Tut, tut, too much coke, my dear. Bite, yes, bite! Want some flesh? Scream yes - yes - Y-E-E-S-S-S-S-S-S!! Brain explodes, cock explodes and eyes slide back into skull.

The girl pushes against Rob with her knee and he rolls onto the floor, pushing himself back up onto his elbows to see her slip out of the door. Andy looks in, takes a step and swings a fist but Rob pulls back confused and the fist only lightly scrapes his chin. He watches it swing again, fascinated as it gathers momentum. As it comes towards him his hand shoots up and locks itself on Andy's wrist and he then pulls hard so Andy crashes on top of him. Rob leaps up, grabbing a small round bedside lamp and holding it high above Andy like a crude club. Andy cowers behind his hands. Rob drops the lamp on the hard floor and it cracks.

'Angela's in fucking tears, you wanker!'

He staggers out to the kitchen where Angela sobs into her friend's shoulder. Her friend looks venom at Rob and holds a knife at him. Then the stereo dies. Then there is a knock at the apartment door and Rob, being nearest, opens it.

Strange, the way she says me name like a question. No surprise, a mere whisper, a defeated end-of-the-world type sound. 'Study' she'd said.

Grabbing his jacket, he pushes past her and down the hall to the lift. He falls in, poking his finger into button G and holding his head in his hands and moaning as the lift hisses down to the street. At the Ground Floor he falls out, reels like an ice skater with temporary loss of control and crashes into the privet hedge that borders the neatly cut lawn. A porter approaches.

'We've got signs up: Keep Off The Grass'

'Fuck off!'

Oxygen floods his brain, he stands and falls backwards again, then regains some semblance of balance.

The way she said me name and her scent in the lift. It didn't – it wasn't - it couldn't have – maybe it just looked like – study, she said, some fucking college.

Reeling like a drunken stilt-walker across the grass and ornamental garden, Rob leaps the small wall, clattering onto the pavement where he shouts for a cab.

Across the river: Baker Street. Bond Street. Hyde Park. Victoria. Kensington. Fulham. Dusk tumbles in electric lights and flashing neon. What do I care? Never watch the world news, care about other peoples wars, read the papers, vote. I have my world and am the envy of many. Out here I feel something: I feel power, destiny, pleasure. Karen won't abandon me. Maybe I'll finally get a motor.

'I see that kid died, eh?' says the cabby.

'What?' says Rob.

'On the news. That gel – she died.'

'What girl?'

'Terrible innit?'

'Yeah' said Rob, shaking his head, 'terrible'

Vauxhall, Kennington, Stockwell, Clapham, Clapham North, Clapham Common, Clapham Junction. I knew a bird had a flat 'round here who sold E's. Took one with her once. Nearly fucking killed me. The only E I ever took that nearly fucking killed me. But it didn't stop me from taking them. Only time I've been afraid of dying. Stuffed six aspirin down me neck and a bottle of vodka. That line of mansions over there, remember that Aussie with too much money and a junkie Daddy? That black girl lives the other way, dope dealer, single Mum, young kid, peddled over-priced grass and worshipped Frank Bruno. I liked her. She spent time taking out the sticks. Whatever happened to her? Was she a friend or just another supplier? Whatever happened to me? Mums and Dads beware when your kids say they want to move to London.

The cab finally pulls up outside a building with a big yellow sign over the door that says POOL.

Come on, Joe. I could just do with a good victory.

XXIV

Rob orders a pint of lager from the bar and then looks around. A dozen large tables, each beneath harsh, naked strip lights, stretch off into the dark, some occupied, most empty. Finding a seat in a booth that overlooks the tables, Rob lights a cigarette. Just then a black face Rob doesn't know appears out of the dark and whispers:

'Hash? Weed?'

Rob glances up casually, nonchalantly.

'Got any acid?'

The face belongs to a body but the body wears the same coloured clothes as the surroundings so it almost looks like a face floating in mid-air.

'Acid? You want acid?'

'Yeah. You know what acid is don't you?'

'How do I know you're not DS?'

'Gimme some weed,' Rob orders.

The face jerks its head in the direction of the toilet. He and Rob go through. The man produces a small bag of grass. Rob puts it to his nose and sniffs it.

'You're having a laugh aren't you?'

'What, man?'

'Fucking parsley!'

'Okay, cool it, man. Look, I give you acid but you can't do it in here right?'

'Let me guess: you're on a profit split with the management and they can tolerate Class B's but not Class A's?'

'You've been around the block, man.'

'Takes one to know one,'

From another pocket the dealer produces another plastic bag of green. Rob sniffs the second packet.

'That's more like it. Gimme some skins as well. What's the score on puffing in this gaff?'

'Not wise if they don't know your face' says the dealer, peeling off half a dozen papers and giving them to Rob.

'Fair enough. What about these trips?'

The dealer drops two tiny cardboard squares into Rob's palm. Rob is suspicious but the dealer says 'Trust me' so he pays and the dealer exits the toilet first. Rob looks down at the tiny squares and wonders if he's been ripped off but he doesn't care that much.

Years ago, when I was a virgin, I'd get screwed by twats peddling me lumps of wood covered in boot polish, telling me it's hard and I'd hand over me entire fucking giro. Then I'd discover I'd been screwed and spend the next fortnight starving to death 'coz, like Fat Freddy says: 'Drugs get you through times of no money better than no money gets you through times of no dope'. For a druggie its better to take drugs than it is to eat. Ten quid for two trips ain't gonna break me fucking bank and who knows - they might even be the real thing!

He puts them on the tip of his tongue and swills a mouthful of lager around in his mouth, taking care to swallow the two squares down in one. Then he squeezes into a cubicle, locking the door behind him. He sticks three of the cigarette papers together and then licks along the seam of the cigarette. He peels a strip off and crumbles the tobacco out onto the skins. His expert fingers lift this and roll it between finger and thumb to spread the tobacco out evenly. Then Rob sprinkles the weed from the bag onto the tobacco. Finally, he picks up the open joint between fingers and a thumb and rolls it into a tight tube. One end he nips over and into the other end he inserts a tiny rolled-up piece of cardboard from the edge of his cigarette packet. He puts the spliff into his inside pocket, finishes his lager in some gulps and then walks outside onto the street. He smokes his spliff there, knowing that he is now about to touch his own personal nirvana. In the next few hours he'll drink as heavily and as hard as he can and stick as much dope into his body as is possible in the certain knowledge that his reality will be seriously altered, if only for a short time. What he has already shoved into his body over the course of that weekend was hair of the dog, something to tide him over, to temporarily block reality. Now it was time for a serious does of abuse to escalate into a trance-like state of idiocy.

The smoke is good. It embeds into him, making the dusk of the evening shimmer and blend into a series of rich and languid colours. He tokes three or four times in succession on the spliff, each time trying to find some hidden part of his lungs that has never been touched by smoke before, so the dope can slip into his bloodstream and pummel his brain. But this mission is not successful and when he exhales he doesn't feel any more stoned than normal so he flicks the roach into the gutter and goes back inside, ordering another lager to quench his thirst. Just then Joe walks in. They touch fists.

'Sorry I'm late, Rob, business. You know how it is.'

'Are you late?'

'Rack 'em up!' says Joe, buying a lager and ordering some cues.

Rob selects a discreet table in a far corner and pours the balls into the triangle on the green baize. He positions the white as Joe approaches the table with two cues and a pint of lager. He hands one of the cues to Rob and says: 'Fire away!'

Rob takes careful aim and then slams the white into the pack, scattering them off the three side cushions, watching two yellows and one red fall into the back pockets.

'You jammy cunt!'

Choosing yellows, Rob slams down two more before settling for a good position on the third. Joe looks around the table for his best option.

'What you been up to today?'

'Not much' says Rob.

'Nothing to report?'

'Not really.'

'How'd you get on with that septic?'

'What septic?'

'Yesterday, said you was poking some yank fond of S & M?'

Yesterday? A zillion years away is yesterday, Joe.

Joe shoots but misses.

You're not concentrating, Joe. Lack of concentration can prove very expensive in the long run. I am not in the mood to take prisoners tonight. I am not in the mercy mood.

Rob sinks two more in quick succession and then starts on the black.

'Fuck! Looks like a fucking whitewash!'

Fuck. I felt a little tingle just then. Like a little thermal lance probing me insides. Have I got the real thing here or is it just me imagination?

Joe rises to the challenge and sinks three reds, balancing the number of colours on the table a little more but only delaying the inevitable.

'Come on, Joe!'

Rob slams down the black like a cannonball. He straightens his back to seek Joe's resignation to a crushing defeat but Joe has backed away from him and something frightening has flashed across his face. His eyes aren't looking at Rob but past him so Rob instinctively turns and finds himself face to face with two men. One of them he recognises – an oriental man with a light grey jacket and black straight, shoulder-length hair. The other man is older, middle-aged, in his fifties. He has lost most of his hair and what is left sprouts silver above each ear. He too wears a suit but apart from that there is nothing noticeable about his face. He has an anonymous face, a face that would slip healthily and discreetly into any background due to the physiological fact that his features appear to be constantly changing.

'Nice shot,' says this figure, sincerely as well.

Rob turns back to Joe and says: 'You know them?'

The older guy speaks with the authority of a Boss.

'Thank God we can always rely on our mates to sell us out eh? After all, what are friendships for but to corrupt? Well, the traditional approach didn't work did it? I believe you've already met my partner here, Mr Chang, though you haven't been formally introduced. I know how you got out of your flat by the way. Ambitious that. Takes guts. I wish I'd had a fucking camera!'

He swears in a south London accent. He's a gangster of sorts, a criminal. Oh fuck. My guts. Them trips. What's happening to me vision?

'Sorry, Rob, but it's for the best!' mumbles Joe.

Rob clutches his pool cue like a weapon and waits.

Mr Gangster takes a few steps towards him on one side of the table and Mr Chang on the other.

'You know, I like to think I'm a bit like Sainsbury's or Safeway's - the march of progress. All those little high street corner shops of yesteryear, they're history now. Nostalgia don't pay see? Got to think big, all encompassing, all enveloping. There's no room for the independents, the mavericks, the lone operators. Those gangster days of Al Capone are long gone but there's no sense in destroying the opposition, don't you think?'

At this Mr Gangster places something on the edge of the pool table. Rob looks at it –it's his mobile.

'So, my offer is a fair one. Do as your friend here and join the firm.'

The mobile rings. The four men look at it. Mr Smith nods his head once. Rob picks it up and connects.

'Rob? It's George. Just to let you know I got a bit of news on that Bob Sharp geezer's been tagging you: it's Old Bill, mate. Some bird popped her buttons on E a few days back and the cops want get a result to keep the press happy. Don't ask me how I know, I just know. Watch your back mate okay? Rob? You there, Rob?'

Mr Gangster takes the mobile, looks at the tiny screen and presses the button that breaks the connection but Rob speaks first: 'And if I don't?'

XXV

I'm black inside, like oil, like coal. I know that now. I've a black soul and a black heart - I can see that. I can see that in the state of the wound in me left side. I peel away the cloth of me shirt. It's red, blood soaked round the tear where the knife came through. The wound is pumping red, a living thing, pulsing with every heartbeat, trickling out and spreading slowly down me left side. I never really respected me body before but this has been a sobering experience. Deep, deep in the heart, in the exact centre of the wound is nothing but blackness. And that proves I've a black interior and stumbling, mumbling and fumbling, the acid is eating into me head, turning everything inside out. That punch in the face and then the knife, they all took a toll that reality will tell me is serious but I'm not in reality now. Thank fuck I'm not in reality now.

I slip down the stairs under the lines and come up again on the other platform of Clapham Junction. It's quiet and there are few people. I manage to make it to a bench where I perch on the edge with me legs shaking. I'm feeling weak. Me brain is sending messages to me body to respond but the body is sluggish and slow. It's unreal. People gawp at me but of course this is London and nobody wants to get involved. They don't want to notice me. They don't want to give attention to somebody else. They want others to look at them. They want others to point at them and give them special attention instead. They're bored see? They lead boring lives. They kid themselves they're special, that something's going on that can't be happening anywhere else.

The train, all neon and chrome and light, slides along the platform and its doors hum open. I manage to make it to a seat, aware the left side of me jeans is heavy with blood. I can feel it squelching in me boots. As the train rolls on to Victoria I spy a young girl in the next carriage. She looks preoccupied, talking away like she's on a personality disorder trip, let out from the farm under heavy medication. She takes a packet of Johnnies out of her bag and a safety pin. I don't think she can see me watching her meticulously stabbing the pin through the packet time after time.

The acid is burrowing into me inner being with warm tendrils. I think I'll roll up on the floor into a tight ball and dream of the Cleveland Hills when I would walk for hours through fields and climb the steep paths up to Chop Gate and stand on the cliff edge looking down across the Tees Valley from Darlington in the west to the shores of the North Sea in the east and with my arms wide and the howling wind blowing tears of joy across me cheeks cry: 'All – this - is - mine . . .'

www.ingramcontent.com/pod-product-compliance
Lightning Source LLC
Chambersburg PA
CBHW071429180526
45170CB00001B/270